Inspirational Stories

*S*that
Spark
Our Emotions
and Touch the

Heart and Soul

Inspirational Stories
that
Spark
Our Emotions
and Touch the
Heart and Soul

Pam Fiecke

CITI OF
BOOKS

CITIOFBOOKS, INC.
3736 Eubank NE Suite A1
Albuquerque, NM 871113579
www.citiofbooks.com
Hotline: 1 (877) 3892759
Fax: 1 (505) 9307244

Ordering Information:

Quantity sales. Special discounts are available on quantity purchases by corporations, associations, and others. For details, contact the publisher at the address above.

Printed in the United States of America.

ISBN13:   Softcover   979-8-89391-010-0
                    eBook   979-8-89391-011-7

Library of Congress Control Number: 2024905248

All Bible quotes taken from King James Version

TABLE OF CONTENTS

Every New Beginning Starts With A New Adventure (January)

Love Is The Greatest Gift Of All Because It Can Be Given To Others In Many Different Ways (February)

Springtime, A Time To Rejuvenate And Feel Fresh Again (March)

Sharing Our Talent And Messages With Others (April)

Sometimes We Wonder About The World Around Us (May)

Summertime, A Time Of Learning And Discovery (June)

Our World Consists of Many Good Things But, Setting a Good Example Outlives them all (July)

Our Surroundings Bring On A New Perspective (August)

Introduction

In this life, everyone has a choice to make about being a friend to God or to be his foe.

We can serve God or we can serve the devil. We all know we live in a world of trials and temptations. We also know we can over come and with stand the devil and his ways.

Everyday we will encounter the devil nipping at our heels. We as strong Christians need to take a stand and refuse to be destroyed by the entanglement of his snares.

We may falter at times being imperfect human beings but, with faith and endurance we can come from our bended knees and stand strong by fixing our eyes on Jesus. Jesus is there for all of us in good times and in difficult times.

You will read a host of Inspirational Stories, written in creativity, that will arouse your curiosity, will educate, encourage, and will touch your heart and soul in a most meaningful way.

We have been created and designed for the purpose of connecting with God and to SERVE Him with our hands, voice, and feet.

We are here to touch the lonely, serve the poor, and help the sick.

We are here to Evangelize- spread the word of Jesus, to up-lift and be compassionate to others.

We are to live as an example of Jesus and to lead the way, step by step and to light the path for others.

In Honor And Dedication

In our lifetime there have been many people who have helped us, cared for us, brought happiness to our day and simply left an inspiring mark on our heart and soul that never subsides or leaves us.

They have given us good direction and guided us to success in a healthy way of living. They encourage us to go on and be the best we can be with our God-given talents.

I, would like to acknowledge my family, friends, neighbors, high school Teacher, and the surrounding communities for all they have done to help me along life's journey.

A special Thank You to Chloe Bennett, Elijah Mari, Angelique Mendoza and Maria Torres of Citi of Books, Inc., from Albuquerque, NM.

Citi of Books gave me a wonderful direction, a positive outlook and guidance to all of my many questions and concerns. They were very patient striving for the best for any Author. Citi of Books made me feel comfortable and confident at all times when talking to them. They were very amazingly proactive in all the work they did along the way.

In Honor, I have respectfully Dedicated my 1st edition Novel, in 2008, "Inspirational Stories that Spark Our Emotions and Touch the Heart and Soul."

To the following:

My former English Teacher — Robert D. Henning (Lester Prairie Public School)

My former Priest, Msgr. Robert J. Wyffels (Winsted Holy Trinity Church)

The Herald Journal, in Winsted, MN CEO/Publisher — Chris Schultz

General Manager — Dale Kovar
HJ/ED editor & staff — Lynda Jensen
In Honor, I have respectfully Dedicated my 2nd edition Novel, in 2021, "Inspirational Stories that Spark our Emotions and Touch the Heart and Soul."

To the following:

My former English Teacher — Robert D. Henning (Lester Prairie Public School)

The Herald Journal, in Winsted, MN CEO/Publisher — Chris Schultz

General Manager — Dale Kovar
Sign Dept. Manager – Troy Feltmann
Friend – Sarah Franke
Friend – Diane Gustad

In Honor, I have respectfully Dedicated my 3rd edition Novel, in 2024, "Inspirational Stories that Spark Our Emotions and Touch the Heart and Soul."

To the following:

My former English Teacher – Lester Prairie Public School – D. Henning

The Herald Journal, in Winsted, MN CEO/Publisher — Chris Schultz

General Manager — Dale Kovar

Managing Editor – Andrew Meuleners

Sales – Jason Blashack

Friend – Sue Dressel

Friend – Sarah Franke

Friend – Diane Gustad

Thank You for helping me along my journey in life, and for sharing your moments of kindness to me in all ways imaginable!

Every New Beginning Starts With A New Adventure

(January)

Stories Spark Our Emotions

Dedicated in Honor
(To: The Herald-Journal of Winsted, MN)
(Publishing Company)

People of all ages in life, enjoy telling or writing stories and there's a variety of ways in which we have all found to do that for others. Stories can inspire you, some can touch your soul, some can make you smile, giggle, or perhaps bring on a hardy laugh.

There are stories that, when told, can shift your mind-set, open your heart, hold your family closer and your friends a little tighter.

Some stories can open your thinking to new possibilities. Some can stimulate your desire and create a brighter tomorrow. Then there are stories that find you searching for a solution.

Some stories may even display a little darkness, bring tears to your eyes, or an ache to your heart.

We, at times, may even think of ourselves as being artists. Each of us paints a different picture every day on our own individual canvas, from morning to sundown, in hopes that it will be filled with hope and cheerfulness. We then flip the page over and start a new picture for the next day.

We all need to learn that our life experiences, if written or told before others, can teach many valuable lessons to mankind. Jesus was our perfect example and role model. He went out into the world and told stories.

Amazingly, all these stories were compiled and put into book form.

Interesting to find, not one of these stories was written in the context of "once upon a time."

This storybook was, and still is today, called the Bible.

The Bible in today's world means something different to most everyone, but to a Christian, it's our roots, spiritual nourishment, guidance, and source of daily living.

It guides and directs people, it strengthens and upholds. It brings an out-pouring of faith and joy to mankind.

It's a sharp tool for obedience, yet Jesus' arms are wrapped around each and every human being that he created.

None of us will ever live a life eliminating struggles, trials or temptations.

Nor do any of us live carefree, perfect lives.

In others words, how we climb up the mountain is just as important as how we get down the mountain.

For many of us life becomes one gigantic test followed by one gigantic lesson.

It's how we accept winning and losing, good luck and bad luck, as well as darkness and the light.

Through it all, Jesus has promised to walk with us every step of the way. God, however, has not promised to live our lives for us. He is not walking ahead of us, or behind us. He's walking beside us and guiding us through life's problems; with his arms gently around us.

In all the twists and turns, and the ups and downs in life, he's taking our hand and guiding us to his purpose in life. It's been said that his ways are better than our ways. Jesus was a teacher and still is our best teacher today.

To take a glance at Jesus in his direction is a positive step for any person.

With great hope, Jesus has called us to order our lives around his priorities and purpose. So that we, too, can be a true example of his people in the world…not of the world.

Everything Has A Beginning

Everything we do in life has some sort of a beginning.

Every year, we start with the month, of January. We pace through every month and in no time at all we are back to the beginning. We all know we have to start somewhere.

Most writers will tell you they started with a blank piece of paper. In school perhaps a teacher laid a piece of paper on your desk and said to the class, "write whatever comes to your mind, try to be creative." In the beginning you starred at the blank piece of paper. Nothing seems to come into your mind. All you saw was a blank sheet of paper, with holes on the side.

Your mind rushed and many ideas jumble together, leaving you in frustration.

It's hard to separate all the many things you want to express. You now realize that the onset of writing was more then you expected.

Little by little thoughts, ideas, and creativity come into focus.

You realize writing takes on a different perspective. It takes thinking, determination, and a positive attitude.

Most importantly, it takes courage to write. This is called the muscular part of writing.

In time, the pen in your hand and the words written on your paper will flow through you.

Anything that has real and lasting value is always a gift from within. God has sealed each and everyone of us with a touch of his goodness.

In today's world the respect and empathy for another human being is starting to tarnish. Some people have no sense of who other people are. There's a kind of withering away of human sensibility, and this leads to the collapse of our society at a whole.

However, there are people who find that ray of hope and extend it to others in our world and find solutions everyday.

Our conclusion is that whenever two or more people come together in the spirit of harmony it's like putting lightning in a bottle. We laugh. We become excited. Life feels joyous, without drudgery.

When this happens, a difference can be made in the lives of so many people throughout our world.

Amazing things happen when people come together for the same purpose or intent. There is a pull inside each and everyone of us to make a difference while we are here.

It's up to us, to make our time and choices matter.

Our Desires Do Not

Define Us... Our Choices Do

———————— ————————

As we start the beginning of the new year, we are all looking for new ways to upgrade somewhere within our life.

We may even question ourselves, what needs a little bit more focus or attention within our day or perhaps our life style.

The real element in life is understanding that we all need to believe in something, before we can truly stand for it.

God's written Word-not culture, not experience, not tradition… no, the Bible-is the only trustworthy guide for faith and practice.

Scripture clearly shows that throughout time, God has imparted to man the authority to speak of scripture and to exercise the evidence of our seeking truth by shielding the Bible righteously. (2 Timothy 3:16) "All scripture is given by inspiration of God, and is profitable for doctrine, for reproof, for correction, for instruction in righteousness."

We know from scripture that God is the judge of all. However, according to the Bible, the act of protecting, promoting, and shielding in behalf of the Bible righteously is a benefit to the individual Christian and to the body of believers, as a whole.

In fact, the word of God says that God enables man to speak, commands man to speak, and is pleased with those who seek to shield God's written words of the Bible. This also makes us an effective witness for Christ, and is a demonstration of God's grace to others.

Our choices either make us a slave to sin or a slave to Christ. By our willful choices in our lives, we either become more Christ- like or less Christ-like. What we do, no what we desire makes us who we are.

We are all surrounded everyday by sin. It's that step that we take that determines our reaction-to walk away from sin or be surrounded in it.

In the hearts of everyone, may God turn the compass in every human heart to the direction to protect, promote, and shield God's written words.

God's written words are not interchangeable. They do not become old fashion, they do not fade away, nor do they become something that we should walk away from.

They are written for us to protect and shield at all times and in all circumstances. They are of truth, of guidance, and a source to our everyday life style.

Being a Christian is about taking a journey together, in well focused healthy steps with our mind, body, heart, and soul.

We need to strive to be the best that we can be in any situation that comes before each and everyone of us.

We need to preserve what God has implemented and laid before all of us.

Within each and everyone of us, we have desires. Some are healthy desires and some are not.

It's what we do with our choices of those desires that define us.

Everyday we will be faced with many situations. We just need to caution ourselves to those individual choices in life.

May we learn, as we go on our journey in life, to develop healthier ways within our day and become the best that each one of us can be.

Believe In Yourself

Dedicated in Honor
To: Jason Blachack of Lester Prairie, MN
(Sales Rep. of the Herald Journal in Winsted, MN)

When you believe in yourself, you are not afraid to dare and experience life.

Each one of us is unique and has talents that no one else has. It is up to us to use our talents to bear fruit, otherwise they will go to waste. By sharing our talents with others, they will reproduce themselves.

Others perceptions of you and their actions to put holes in your dreams, do not matter as long as you remain true to yourself.

It will not matter what skin color you have. It will not matter your age.

It will not matter who your parents are. It will not matter what sex you are.

It will not matter where you are employed.

It will not matter what you drive, where you live, or your financial status.

However, what will matter is that you need to believe in yourself.

We need to remember respectfully that we are, "One Nation under God."

We have the responsibility to help others in all causes and to preserve and protect humanity.

When you have faith in what you are doing, your plan will benefit.

When you have a mission statement, goals, objectives in place, your plan will benefit.

When your works are of value and ethical to those around you, your plan will benefit.

When you use your ability to create better lives and educate people, your plan will benefit.

When you use your talents, cultivate them and put them at the service of humanity, your plan will benefit.

When you respectfully put your customers needs first, your plan will benefit.

When you provide a positive, "I can do that for you!" And a positive attitude, a huge smile, open arms to serve, within your day, your plan will benefit.

Most importantly, when you are God centered and not self centered, your plan will benefit.

That is why it is necessary for us to go out there and experience life. Do not be scared to take risks. Do not be afraid to open a new door.

Believe in yourself as, you never know what may be waiting for you behind it.

We need to get to know ourselves and learn to assess our weaknesses and strengths.

Those who are afraid of the unknown are not moving forward, they are standing still.

Open that new door, because, you do not want to spend the rest of your life wondering what might have been if you had just had faith in yourself.

Make sure to turn on the light!! Do not be like the servant in Matthew 25, entrusted with one talent. He believed so little in himself that he did not allow his talent to bear fruit.

As the Lord entrusted talents to his servants according to their abilities, whatever your mission in life or whatever talent given to you by your creator, it is given to you according to your ability.

We need to implement self confidence and discover our strengths and learn to go in forward motion carrying our light upon life's journey.

Remember that whatever life challenges you with, you are well equipped to wrestle with it. All you have to do is, believe in yourself!

Trying To Do Good

It was one of those typical winter days when the weather was clouded, sleeting, raining, accompanied by high winds.

Trevor, 10 years old, sat by the living room window and watched the beastly, chilly weather beat against the living room window.

A shiver came to his body causing him to tremble.

Trevor was bored. He wanted something fun to do. He sat and thought for a moment. He had a wonderful idea.

He went running to the kitchen drawer and pulled out one of his mom's favorite cook books. "I'll bake something." He enthusiastically said to himself.

He pushed a chair against the counter top.

Opening the cupboard door he found a big mixing bowl and a measuring cup.

He got off the chair and pulled open a utensil drawer. All the many different things he could stir with. This was exciting!

Looking at the recipe book, he found a cake he wanted to bake. It was called a, "never fail cake", "how perfect," He said to himself.

He started to read, the directions read, "preheat the oven."

He specifically remembered his mother saying, "do not touch the oven dials when I'm not home."

He thought to himself, "I'll get everything ready and mom can put it in the oven for me when she gets home."

He dashed with excitement to the pantry closet. Looking from shelf to shelf he found the flour way up on the top shelf.

He pushed his chair in front of the pantry closet. He crawled up upon the chair.

The flour container looked very heavy. He gripped his fist together and flexed a muscle. "I can do it." He reassured himself.

Reaching for the flour container it toppled onto the floor. The container lid flew off and flour clouded the kitchen floor.

The dog was frightened and made his tracks threw the flour leaving foot prints.

Trevor looked at the mess and sighed. He lifted the flour container onto the counter. It was easier to handle being half empty.

He scooped some flour into the measuring cup and poured it into the mixing bowl.

He then measured some sugar and vanilla into the mixing bowl. He then measured the cocoa, into the bowl it went. This was fun!

He had a mountain forming in his bowl.

His shirt was covered in flour, sugar, and cocoa. He giggled. He knew that what he wore was washable.

Reaching for the eggs in the refrigerator, his puppy returned wagging his tail and licking Trevor's hands, making him drop the eggs, that he had in his hands onto the floor.

He then slipped in the eggs and landed in the white and yellow sticky egg mess.

There he sat with big crocodile tears. He got himself up.

His mother opened the front door to see a huge mess, including her son's clothing. She was astounded.

He was sure a scolding was coming.

She questioned Trevor, "what are you doing and what are you making?"

He responded, "I was trying to make you a cake. I was trying to surprise you by doing something good."

She proceeded to get another spoon to help him mix the batter. Softy she said. "The oven isn't turned on. You are a good listener.

Sometimes we try to do something good in life and it turns into a mess.

Just because we might mess up, we can't stop trying to do good for God and others. Sooner or latter we'll get it right and then they'll be glad we tried."

Trevor looked at his mother and questioned, "is that why they call it a "never fail cake?"

Love Is The Greatest Gift Of All Because It Can Be Given To Others In Many Different Ways (February)

The Greatest Gift To Another Is Love

When we flip the page of our calendar over from January to February our thoughts embrace the word love.

Valentine's Day is considered that heart-filled day.

We enthusiastically find genuine ways to extend our love from our heart to another loved one.

Some send cards, some buy flowers, some buy jewelry, and some drape themselves in romance.

We purchase chocolate candy, heart shaped window clings, stuffed "I love you" pillows and ceramic momentous.

Stores, magazines and television commercials extend their encouragement and direct us to many products to be purchased and given in love.

February is the month that brings people's focus to love. Love is the prime motivator in life.

Each of us have come into this world to give our love away to somebody.

To treat others with love regardless of who they are, what they do or what they are unable to do.

Speak to them in a way that opens their heart to feel wanted, needed and of value.

In other words, treat others like you would like to be treated.

When we learn to be present with others in loving ways, we will feel cooperation, harmonizing, forgiveness, and acceptance that will be anchored to our soul with the essence of love.

15

Love has so many different descriptions and duties within a day.

Sometimes love wants to touch you, embrace you, then love finds a way to lift your spirit.

Love will never leave you. Love will never dishonor. Love will never take anything from you.

Love is the voice of God whispering to you from within yourself.

Love comes to visit each and everyone of us personally. Love works around the clock.

Love has no set time.

Love has many concerns of how you feel, why you feel the way you do, and what can I do to make you feel better.

Love wants you to know that God watches and his love is always available to you.

Through God's love we are cared for and protected. God will smother us in his love for healing our biggest hurt.

Love doesn't give-up.

Love spreads from one person to another. Love is without end. Jesus didn't love by sending us a fancy card, heart shaped balloons,

chocolate candy, or a bouquet of flowers.

What he did give was His life. He bought our redemption with His own blood, not because it was His obligation. It was because He loved us completely.

This Bible passage proves God gave the greatest gift of love ever known to mankind.

You won't find any other Bible passage in the Bible that clearly spells out "Valentine" than this one. John 3:16

"For God so lo(V)ed the word,

that he g(A)ve

His on(l)y

begott(e)n So(n,)

(t)hat whosoever

believeth (I)n him

should(n)ot perish,

but have (e)everlasting life."

Love Can Be Given In Many Ways

A week before Valentine's Day a mother decided it was time for her children to assume some responsibility. She laid out a box of Valentines on her kitchen table for her children.

They were to send them to whomever they wanted to. The mother smiled and replied, "When you are finished all three of you may go to the post office."

When the children got to the post office, they laid down all their envelopes. The spirited child blurted out to the post office lady, "We got to mail Valentines this year, to whomever we wanted to."

The post office lady laughed and replied to all three of the children, "Valentine's Day is a times for giving our love to whomever we want to, that is a choice for everyone. Did you know that love can be given in many different ways?"

All three of the children giggled. "The oldest child spoke, "That is why we are here. My mom and dad love each other." The post office lady chuckled.

"OK, that is true, but do you three love each other all the time?"

The middle child spoke up, "no, we fight and argue. Timmy took my truck. It was my favorite toy and he wouldn't share. Then Bobbie spilled juice on my new shirt. Was I mad!"

The oldest child intervened, "We all argue at my house, but we forgive and then we forget."

The post office lady smiled. The spirited child reaching into his pocket then said "I have this Valentine and I sent it to the most

17

important person in the world this year. I want you to check and see if everything is alright with it."

The spirited child sent a Valentine to: "God the Father, He lives in heaven. Just follow His path and you will find Him waiting for you. I love Him, trust Him, and want to be His forever. PS I don't have a numbered address a zip code or stamp on it because none is needed."

The post office lady responded to the spirited child, "No more Valentines like this are ever needed because we are all covered by God's great love if we believe in Him. Without question, God is love."

The spirited child said "I'm still going to fold my hands and whisper all my troubles and thank Him for all the good He does for me."

The post office lady smiled and replied "That's what we are all supposed to do." The three of them left the post office together, holding hands.

An Expression Of Love

Valentine's Day is one of those most special days when we should find the time to reflect our love to another person.

On Valentine's Day the word "love" will be used in a variety of ways, and more than usual. In today's world, we have many different ways to do just that: a special card, flowers, dining out for the evening, a trip away, jewelry, a hug, a box of candy, a phone call, a hand colored picture to be hung on the fridge, or perhaps a soft spoken message of appreciation to another.

There are millions of ways to send a message of love to another person. May we all find the time to individually express our own personal ways of knitting another person closer to our heart.

One of the most wonderful attributes about knowing God is that there is always so much more to know and so much more to discover.

Just when we least expect it, he surprises us about who he is and how he works.

We sometimes may even question his ways and even scramble with what he has challenged us with.

Yet we know without question God is love. If we stop and think about his love for a moment, we will discover that God's love encompasses the whole world and then, in the next on-going thought, we realize he can also be so small that he wraps himself around our heart, bringing joy into our lives.

However, nothing will ever be able to separate us from the love of God demonstrated by our lord Jesus Christ when he sacrificed all he had and all he was by dying on the cross for each one of us.

Jesus didn't only talk about love: he lived and died in a very profound and concrete way of example.

As we respectfully pause for a moment, may our heart and mind connect as we ponder these words, as Christ drew near to death,

he, himself, trembled. It was an agonizing experience displayed to all his creations.

He never felt such excruciating pain, such abandonment, even from his father, to his humanity, his assumed flesh. It seemed torturing as they bore witness; but he passed into it, just for the love of us.

He even died for those who rejected him, just for the love of us.

There is no greater love than Jesus' love. In reality it takes years to build up trust, and just seconds to destroy that seal of trust. By his great example, we love because he first encountered an outpouring of sacrifice for all, giving a permanent meaning to the world around us.

He was, and still is today, our central figure of trust and love.

Loving The Elderly

One of my fondest memories as a child was being around my grandparents. I loved going for walks and talks with my grandpa, hand-in-hand, or putting my fingers around the loop that was sewn on the side of his old fashion bib overalls.

My discovery was that the elderly always took big steps while walking, but they were slow steps. I took many little steps, but they had to be fast to keep up.

It always averaged out to where we could keep up with each other.

My grandmothers were always good with baking home-made bread or coffee cake. The kitchen always smelled wonderful.

My grandparents were a joy to listen to, though it was a long ways up for my eyes to see them while they spoke. They always made sure that I learned something from them when I was with them.

They had very caring hearts, and they made me feel special at any given time throughout the day.

As time went on, the roles reversed. I walked with fast steps, and now they looked up to see me speak.

Instead of them caring more so for me, I had to care and watch their safety for them.

However, none of that ever stopped the joy and laughs we shared together. What I thought to be caring wasn't even a start to the underlining of what deep caring can be.

Eventually, we became their hands and feet for them.

We became their housekeepers, lawn caretakers, and every other aspect we never imagined possible.

We begin to realize there's time involved, but we make every effort to be at their side to make things comfortable for them.

What matters most is that we put our Christian faith into practice. We need to keep in mind that we are spending our last days together. We too will become old some day, some of us sooner than others.

Most of us have visited a Nursing home or an Assisted living home. This brings a new challenge to our attention, namely, focusing on the needs of our elderly in a dignified manner, remembering who they are as individual humans.

What always strikes me is the way the residents reach out for you, wordlessly begging you to take their hands, to talk to them, to treat them like they are special. Some residents are left in these homes without family or friends although, it doesn't matter to the residents that you didn't come to visit them. You don't need to know them, and they don't need to know you.

What matters to them, is that you are there.

Someone who is paralyzed can love with their eyes. Someone who is blind can love with their voice and their touch.

We need to touch the hearts of the elderly. In a short time, if you pay close attention, you will see a love shown back to you, in a way you never thought possible.

This is a rare and genuine unspeakable human love, a true experience of what real love for each other as humans is all about.

God Has Given Us The Greatest

Demonstration Of Love

February is considered the month of love. Everywhere you go you see the colors red and white.

You see hearts in all shapes and sizes. There are messages of love expressed on cards, balloons, candy boxes, flower arrangements, stuffed animals, and ceramic momentous.

All the red hearts displayed in any manner are beautiful. They are perfect and show know sign of impurities, bumps, bruises, scrapes, or scares.

For a moment if we examined the reality of a human heart we would be amazed to find the exact opposite.

We, being humans take everything to heart. Our heart beats everyday. Our heart also takes on a beating we sometimes can't fathom.

We all encounter happiness and excitement. Our heart beats in joyous accord.

There are times when we run into disappointment. Our heart is bruised by the news that we don't want to hear or see.

When spoken too in harshness, our heart may show signs of being broken.

Our heart may have jagged and frayed edges from all the severed disrespectful words shared. It takes a long time to mend a wounded heart.

Then there are some who have a closed heart. They choose not to give or to receive.

Then we have those who are receptive to giving, sharing, caring and loving. There heart blossoms with joy when being around others. Then we have those who have a chunk of their heart missing. A loved one has left them or some type of loss has occurred. The loss
seems to great to bear.

Then we have those who have a heart that is blanketed because someone found the time to gently cover the heart with the warmth of their comforting words.

Then we have people who look at others and say, "you have a heart of gold."

If we could all see each others heart in good times and difficult times we'd be astounded by the looks of another ones heart.

We all have one other avenue, the greatest source of all.

When we are alone at our utmost saddest and loneliest moment in the darkest hours of the night, it's then, God's love can be intimately found.

He knows how to soothe our broken heart. In time he mends our heart, for he knows a part of us has died.

He doesn't care how the heart looks for, when we pour out our hurt to him, he in return pours His love inside each and everyone of us. He comes to us and repairs the bumps, bruises, scrapes, scares, and all that needs tending too.

In time our heart takes on a new look because God deeply cares and loves each and everyone of us in the turmoil and wreckage of our day.

He's always waiting and ready with arms open wide to help us all in our time of need.

Springtime, A Time To Rejuvenate And Feel Fresh Again (March)

THE ART OF COMMUNICATION

Most of us have had the experience of trying to communicate with someone who doesn't speak English.

While it's stressful and a bit frustrating, we're usually able to send some clear messages.

We do it mostly with our hands and by pointing and making other gestures, and with our facial expressions.

It's called body language. This was the first method of communication used by our ancestors. Imagine going through this each day of your life without being able to speak to those around you. Just think how boring and lifeless that could have been.

That's what early humans had to do. They also realized they came up short in articulating needs and feelings. They grew tired of just pointing and getting excited looks on their faces. They wanted to communicate in more specific ways.

The next process was the drawing of pictures. Whether people had great artistic talent or not, they could send a message with a more precise meaning by sketching drawings on the ground or on the cave walls. Even the stick figures we draw today would have worked.

Finally, phonics came into place. The development of language became one of the greatest achievements in the history of human race.

Speaking words replaced drawing pictures. We can talk to others and to ourselves in words, but we think in pictures.

What we are doing most of the time when we are talking to another person is exchanging pictures. No matter how hard you try a picture will form in your mind.

Words are what we use every day of our lives to connect with the world and the people in it. They're the tools we use to greet, inform, answer, encourage, comfort, praise, celebrate, thank, pray, and laugh. Regardless, if we shout, use sign language, write or push a button, we all need to communicate somehow. Many people have learned in today's world that kind words cost little, but accomplish much. They can even change lives.

Words not only create emotions they create actions and from our actions flow the results of our lives. Words are not only powerful they can have lasting impact.

Some people even use inappropriate words and even hurtful words. We've all had experience with that unfortunately.

The amazing truth is, the real art of conversation is not only to say the right thing in the right place, but far more difficult still, to leave unsaid the wrong thing at the tempting moment.

We all have frustration and anger and when words fly, these are usually words that are reflecting of what's going on inside of us. Our words, even when were trying to hide our feelings, reveal what's stored inside. It will come out but, sometimes it comes out this way and that way.

The greatest message we can all tell ourselves is that God gave us all a heart to use wisely.

Just think for a moment, there's no misinterpreting the language of the heart because love speaks in any language straight from the heart and pulls us al together, never apart.

The human heart feels things the eyes cannot see, and knows what the mind cannot understand. We have choices everyday with our language.

We can put people down or we can lift them up. We can be self-centered and inconsiderate, or we can be respectful, kind and helpful. For the most part, we do these things with the language we choose.

The tone of voice can be just as important, and sometimes more important than, the words we use.

Just think what kind words, a soft tone, and a gentle touch can do when combined. We all have our own way of speaking while trying to send our message.

The most successful people have the art of being a "good finder." A good finder is a person who never fails to find good in another human person when speaking to them or when they are not present.

A "good finder" always finds a positive approach to a situation and lifts up the people he/she associates with. In other words he/ she is a reputable builder.

Trying is still an art of achievement, an avenue of a forward motion, an experience of that situation. Everyday we learn and experience new things through our efforts of communication.

I sometimes wonder what it would be like if every time we would send our message, that we would let no one come to us without leaving us better and happier.

We all take different paths in life, but no matter where we go, we take a little bit of each other everywhere we go.

THE NON-RETURNABLE GIFT

Sometimes it is amazing how our memory bank will take us as far back as to our childhood.

Perhaps we may have even heard many things our parents said, about ourselves when we were born.

For me, what stands out in my mind is that my parents always spoke of me being born with a full head of thick, brown hair, and weighing in at little over four pounds.

When listening to them speak of this tiny little me, the word "survive" would come to my mind and got my attention every time. Thinking back, technology wasn't what they have today.

Many times my parents would speak of a shoe box they would gently place me in, just to see if I would fit, being so tiny. In amazement I did fit, perfectly.

Looking at the shoe box today, it's hard for me to visualize and comprehend myself being that small and surviving. However, being blessed with good health conditions when born eliminated health issues.

Then the most shocking moment came when my daughter was born.

She was exactly double the weight that I was when I was born. Holding my daughter in my arms, it was hard to imagine that I was half of her total weight, when born. To me she was small. This was an eye opener for me.

We have now advanced to technology where babies can be placed in the palm of one's hand and still survive. Some would think that the child would have to have fought hard for his/her own life.

On the other hand, if we think about it, God was in complete control all along.

Each one of us was etched into being, planned for in advance before conception. Etched into whom we all are today.

We are of God's own design brought into life for his own plan. We all have been born for a purpose.

There are those who interfere with God's plan of action by planning abortions.

Each human life, no matter it's stage, has meaning to someone.

A minute, an hour, or to live to be elderly, time doesn't matter for the life that's begun.

Some babies in life touch maybe one soul, or we may share our soul with many.

We all must realize that, God gives us the first breath, and God is the one who takes our last and final breath away in his time, not our time. A time not determined by minutes or hours, but by the purpose for which the life began.

Your creator etched a purpose into your being. You have been born to fulfill that purpose in a away that only you can. In life you will be called to use your gifts and talents that you were given.

The more you reach out in life, the more you will discover you have gifts you never thought you had. Gifts given from God are defined in many different ways. However, we all need to respect the gift of human life in a dignified manner.

Human life is the most precious gift that can ever be given to another person, and should be thought of as a non-returnable, honored gift from God.

Holding On Tight To The Belief In God

S ince the beginning of time, there have been many arguments as to why people believe what they believe.

Some have died or were killed because of their beliefs. The truth is they fought because of their need to make sense of our existence. We need to know that our existence is not the result of some kind of accident or coincidence, but that there is a logical explanation as to why we are here on earth.

The fact that people believe in something gives them a sense of security, a sense of belonging. A good example of people's sense of security is when they believe in God.

God, no matter how you refer to Him in your religion, does marvelous things in people's lives. If He did not exist already, we would have to invent Him. Some of us can even witness the change we have seen in friends and family because of God's way, not our way.

We hold onto God tightly because we do not want to give up the idea of being under His protection. For those of you who believe in God, can you imagine how frightening and empty your life would be without the thought of Him?

Although I have never seen God, I would not trade my belief in Him for any scientific explanation in the world. I need Him in my life. We all need Him in times of trouble, in times of health issues, in times when we just want to commune with Him in the silence of an empty chapel with a lighted candle. We need His comfort, we need His healing, and most important, we need Him beside us every step of the way, to guide us.

For those, who are book readers, you will also find out in your life time, that the Bible is the most inspiring book you'll ever read or have your hands on. It contains everything one needs to know in order to live a well-balanced life. It has all the rules in life.

Sometimes, we may even question, "What does God want from me? What does God expect from me? Where does God want me? Where are you?" Instead of questioning His presence, just affirm that He is beside us at all times when we praise Him and when we cry out for help.

We all need God in our lives, for He is our anchor throughout life. When I admire the beauty of all creation, I cannot imagine our being here as the result of an accident. To me, there is a creator, and that creator is God.

THE UNFORGOTTEN VISION

There was an elderly lady named Bernice. She kept a vision in her soul. No one had believed what she had seen and no one had believed what she heard.

She fervently looked around. There were sorrows, broken hearts that needed to be healed, and mercy needed in this world.

She saw many hearts that were broken and torn by what others had done, only to discover, it was difficult to undo, therefore, love and compassion was needed to help mend the damage that had been done. Bernice felt within that God turned this challenge into a stepping- stone for her journey in life. She also had a strong belief and openly shared it with the world. "I believe, the closest thing to the heart of our

God is helping hurting people."

God loves when we sing and when we pray. He loves when we come together to celebrate His goodness. Nothing pleases God more than when we take care of one of His children.

We all have a heart of compassion. The question is whether our heart is opened or closed. When God puts love and compassion in your heart toward someone, he's offering you an opportunity to make a difference in that person's life. You must learn to follow love. Don't ignore it. Act on it. Somebody needs what you have. You may not fully realize the impact love and compassion can have until you reach out.

Bernice had a vision. Bernice had a prayer within her heart. Bernice had an answer. Bernice had hope. Bernice found compassion, peace and love. Bernice had the touch for human healing. Bernice was gifted.

Bernice soon left a path for others to follow and also her unforgotten words.

When Bernice was at her last hour and laid to rest. The last prayer was respectfully said. The last flower was respectfully laid.

A weeping man kneeling at her grave site, looked up at the Minister and the people in the area and said, "When a good person dies, a thousand lights go out. And it is said, a giant library is lost."

The weeping man buried his face in his hands. The Minister put his hand on the shoulder of the weeping man and replied, "You'll see her soon. It won't be long and then your hearts will meet and your arms will entwine again. For now, just follow the lights a good person left upon the way."

A woman slowly approached the weeping man and knelt down beside him and whispered in his ear.

"I just want to hold you, come on let me hold you, like Bernice would want to do."

The embracing and compassion that Bernice had shared with many brought strength to the souls of many. With God's help she healed many people with her prayers, touch and gentle words. This led others to do the same and has never been forgotten.

Mending A Broken Heart

One day an elderly lady living in a nursing home in her 90's was sitting in her wheel chair.

Her wheel chair was close to the window, she was observing the near by traffic.

She had the gray spiral curly hair, peaked nose, false teeth, that moved her chin outward as she clenched them together.

Her eyes were of a beautiful sky blue. She always wore the same white sweater that draped over her petite boney shoulders.

She loved her sweater as it kept her frail little body warm.

To occupy her day she seemed most content when paging threw a magazine.

She would often tease the staff in her most clever ways. In her gravely voice she said, "I really think you should take me outside and give me a four-wheeler ride." The staff loved her sense of humor.

One day one of the staff noticed that her sweater had a seam that let loose, causing a hole in her sweater.

The staff lady made mention of the noticeable hole to the resident. With all good intentions she told the elderly lady that if it was alright with her she would discard her old sweater and ask if her family

would purchase her a new one.

The elderly lady became disturbed by this remark and raised her voice to defend that which was hers.

In her gravely voice in anger she said, "That sweater is mine. That's all I have left in life. Please don't take that from me too!"

Another staff person could see the distress in the elderly lady.

In compassion the staff lady knelt down beside her and whispered in her ear. "No one will take your sweater. I promise. Would you like me to mend it for you? It won't take me long. It will be as good as new and then you can wear it again."

The elderly lady removed her glasses and slowly wiped a tear from her cheek before it landed in her lap. "Yes, I would like you to mend my sweater."

The staff lady gently proceeded to take the sweater off the elderly lady.

The staff lady quickly went to get some needle and thread.

The staff lady sat down beside the elderly lady and began to mend her sweater. Stitch by stitch, stitch by stitch.

The elderly lady watched the staff lady mend her sweater with love.

A smile came to both of their faces as the sweater was repaired and ready to be put back on her.

The elderly lady said in a happy voice, "Thank-You, I feel better and warm again."

The staff lady gave her a hug and went about her other duties.

All the elderly lady wanted was the warmth of her white little sweater around her and some-thing she could call her own.

Periodically the staff lady would see the elderly lady wearing her sweater that she mended for her.

The staff lady gave mention to the other staff lady whom wanted to discard her sweater that, a few stitches can mend a broken heart.

The other staff lady realized that mending the sweater was the right thing to do for her, than purchasing a new one.

In time the elderly lady was starting to show rapid signs of health deterioration.

She was eventually put on comfort cares. Her wheel chair was pushed to the side and the white sweater draped across the back of her wheel chair. Her foot pedals laid on the seat of her wheel chair.

The elderly lady was very weak and frail and slowly drifting off. It was just a matter of God's time.

The staff lady went and got the sweater and gently unclasped her one hand and placed the sweater in her hand.

Within days the elderly lady passed away.

Her white little sweater gave a dramatic message to all.

"It takes but one compassionate person to mend a broken heart."

Sharing Our Talent And Messages With Others (April)

Sharing Our Message With Others

One day a kindergarten student named Alex approached his teacher before class.

Alex, who was a little hesitant, gave a sigh and then said, "Teacher, our classroom needs something on the walls. All we have are the ABCs and 1,2,3s. There's nothing pretty to look at and it's Easter time."

The Teacher turned her head and looked around her classroom. To her amazement, Alex was right, the classroom had nothing on its walls. They were bare.

Another little student overheard the conversation and walked up to the teacher and rudely said, "Teacher, the walls are just fine. I come here to listen to you that's all I'm here for!"

Alex stood back and was very offended by that remark, this hurt his little feelings. Alex took a deep breath and voiced his opinion, "I come here to listen, do things, and learn!"

The teacher looked at the little girl and said softly, "Allison, Alex is right, there needs to be something on the walls, it's Easter time!" Allison thought for a moment and then she put her hand on Alex's shoulder and whispered in his ear, "Your idea does sound like fun. I'm sorry, Alex." Alex face lit up, he was happy they agreed.

Class had now begun. The teacher announced that she would like the kindergarten class to sit around the big table that she had in her classroom.

Looking at all the students the teacher said, "Today I would like you all to draw and color a picture of something that reminds you of Easter. I would then like you to tell the other classmates what you drew and then we will hang them on the walls when you are finished."

The students were very excited and eager to begin. They all got a blank piece of paper and some crayons. As time went on the teacher started to walk around and glance at what each student was drawing. Walking by one of the students, she started to giggle.

The teacher walked over to the little girl to see what was so funny. The little girl responded right away,"Teacher, I didn't bump Alex. I really didn't. Look teacher, he has a line on his paper and it's crooked. You need to give him another sheet of paper so he can start all over."

Alex just kept on drawing. The teacher knowing Alex ability in previous classroom projects, looked at the little girl and replied, "Alex's paper will be just fine, regardless if he has drawn a straight line or a crooked line." She then gave Alex a big smile.

When all of the students had finished, the teacher asked each student to tell the class what they individually drew and then they would be hung on the wall for everyone to enjoy.

One little boy said,"I drew a bunch of Easter eggs." another one said she drew an Easter basket filled with Easter goodies. Another student said she drew a church because that is where they go on Easter Sunday. The stick people were all of her family.

Several said they drew a beautiful butterfly because butterflies symbolize new life. Many students drew an Easter bunny carrying an Easter basket filled with goods. Another hand full of students drew a table with family members sitting around it while enjoying an Easter dinner.

Next came Alex. Alex looked at his teacher and said softly, "Teacher, I'm not done with my picture." The teacher understood and told Alex to let her know when he was finished. Alex gave a big smile and continued with his picture.

Another boy held up his picture and replied,"I drew a chocolate bunny and put green grass all around him." A little girl blurted out,

"Mine's a girl bunny. She has a beautiful hat and a dress on and frilly socks and I even drew her a purse to carry candy in."

The little boy looked at the little girl and rolled his eyes and chuckled. Then another little boy rolled his eyes and put his hands over his mouth and giggled.

The teacher looked over at Alex and raised her eyebrows. Alex gave a big smile and said, "Yes, teacher, I'm finished!"

Alex began speaking very boldly and with confidence. "I first found me a brown crayon and drew a big crooked cross. Then I found me a white crayon and I drew a white stick figure on the cross, then I forcibly took the black crayon and put a dot on each of Jesus hands and feet. I said to myself while making the markings, "1,2,3, It is finished." "Those were my nails. Then I found me a red crayon and drew something like raindrops from Jesus head down to his feet. That was the blood of Jesus. It was shed for you and for me."

"That," he stated to others at his table, "is Jesus on the cross. He died for me and for you."

We all have a choice in life, to share the message that He promises eternal joy for all who believe in Him. And yet, sometimes we hesitate when we should speak; we falter when we should proclaim. We neglect to trust God for strength to share His Word.

Alex shared the message. In his own way, with his peers, he witnessed. There was no fear, no holding back. Alex knew he wasn't the best artist in his class. To him that didn't matter. He didn't wonder what his classmates would think or consider that his picture might not be good enough to tell the story. It was his message that he wanted to share.

Alex had something to say to his classmates, and he delighted in the sharing. He found it to be of importance to tell his friends about Jesus and His love.

With His Stripes We Are Healed

One Sunday a grandmother brought her 5 year old grandson with her to church.

Sitting very quietly in thought before the service had begun, the grandson gently stepped up upon the kneeler; he wanted a better view of his surroundings.

He got his grandmother's attention right away. She started to observe him more closely. His little arms were perched on the pew in front of him as he leaned forward. His head went to a downward position as he was looking at the foot of the cross.

He was in deep thought, and you could envision that the wheels of his mind were in full motion. His head and eyes were focused and moving up to the top of the cross, then his head slowly turned side to side to look at Jesus hands, nailed to the cross.

He then stepped off the kneeler quietly and sat beside her.

His eyes then focused on a band-aid that he had on the top of his hand.

He proceeded to rub the band-aid softly. In just a few seconds the grandmother received a little tug on her shirt sleeve. She turned and quietly questioned her grandson, "Are you in need of something?"

She leaned over and she could see he wanted to whisper something into her ear. In his tiny little voice he asked, "Grandma, if I climb up the cross by Jesus and put band-aids on his owies, will that make him feel better?"

She whispered back to him,"Jesus owies don't need to be covered. Jesus died on the cross to take our sins away. His owies are a reminder to all of us."

In his tiny little voice he whispered, "Okay, grandma.. I just wanted to know."

The grandmother knew her grandson would have a difficult time understanding, at such a young age, but then she thought for a moment and realized the answer can be very complex to all of us.

In reality, somewhere within our lives we have all encountered a time when we have cut ourselves, whether it be from a sharp knife, paper cut, steel cut, glass cut, etc.

We can even relate with others, the pain of a tiny cut. They sting and they hurt.

In order to prevent infections we all know that wounds need to be healed or properly taken care of.

If you cut yourself, you wash it and put on antibiotic cream and a band-aid over it so that it can properly heal.

If you have a more serious injury, you wrap it and apply pressure and go to a hospital or doctor to receive treatment.

Wounds, regardless of what kind, take time, patience and tending too. Wounds however, do not give healing. They are known to receive healing.

The amazing part comes when we think of Jesus' wounds. We all know and have heard many times the gruesome death he encountered for our sins, just for the love of us.

If we sit and think for a moment, really think hard, the wounds of Jesus are different than our wounds because of who Jesus was.

Jesus bled, was beaten, crucified, and even put to death. Jesus' wounds do not cry out to be covered with gauze or a band-aid or to even be restored to health.

Instead, his wounds give us healing. Jesus wounds are astounding as they cause us to rejoice on our part.

Jesus was wounded that we might be healed. Jesus was punished that we might be free. Jesus gave himself over to suffer in a most profound manner so we might live eternally. Isaiah 53:5 "but he was wounded for our transgressions, he was bruised for our iniquities: the chastisement of our peace was upon him: and with his stripes we are healed." Three nails, held a man to a cross to do a job no other human could do.

We all need to be thankful to God for these life giving wounds.

IT IS FINISHED

No matter our age, we have all made some type of accomplishment within our lifetime. No matter how big, no matter how small.

The artist takes the paint brush and brushes the last stroke of paint on the canvas. The artist stands back, admires the work she has done, puts down her finishing tools, and says, "It is finished."

The elementary student finishes coloring his picture. He proudly hands it to his teacher and says with a smile on his face, "It is finished."

The soloist sings the last song for a performance and feels at ease knowing, "It is finished."

The cabinet maker screws the last of the hinges on the home- maid cabinet he has made. He is happy to see his job is finalized. To the patron he says, "It is finished."

The farmer at harvest time works many nights along with many long hours of being in the field. When he is finished for the season, he parks his equipment in his sheds, he is exhausted and says, "It is finished."

The cook smells the aroma of some of her home-made soup she has prepared. She samples the soup before serving it to her patrons. With a nod of her head she says, "It is finished."

The grandmother embroiders a dresser scarf, she finishes her last stitch. She holds the dresser scarf at a distance and sees the beauty in every stitch. Her thoughts are, "in every stitch there was love." Laying her needle and embroidery hoop to the side she says, "It is finished."

A little boy in need of stitches for a open wound, looks at the nurse with tears in his eyes. The nurse pats him on the back and says to him, "you were very brave." "It is finished," she says as she puts a wrap around his arm to keep it clean to prevent infection.

The elderly put a puzzle together at activity time. They socialize and are of good company to one another. They are delighted and look at each other with accomplishment and say, "It is finished."

Anytime we come to a closure of a project, it makes us feel good inside. We have mastered another goal. We are happy and excited by what we have achieved and by the ending results.

God sent Jesus to us to fulfill a job that no other human could ever do in his place.

Before leaving this earth Jesus knew he was sent here to complete a mission for his father. Jesus was obedient to his father. Jesus came to serve others, his purpose wasn't to be served. He spread the gospel to others. He performed miracles. He healed the sick and touched the wounded. Jesus spread the truth about eternal life and salvation.

Jesus last moments before dying was heart wrenching. His own father abandoned him. The by standers threw things at him. They spit at him. They yelled at him. They cursed at him. The by standers even walked away from him.

It was his death which completed his work in this world. Without Jesus' death the job his father sent him to do would not have been completed. It would have been an unfinished job.

Jesus announces that his work was completed. John 19:30. When Jesus had received the vinegar, he said, "It is finished: and he bowed his head, and gave up the ghost."

By dying on the cross our redemption was paid in full for the forgiveness of our sins.

God's plan was obediently accomplished by Jesus. It was completed, to what no other human could have done, to the fullest in any other way.

Jesus Found Great Love For All

One day while shopping in a mall, following all the many stores I went to, just to buy a few items, I came across a bench in the mall.

The bench looked so inviting that I decided to rest a few minutes to catch my breath and relax before venturing on.

An elderly man approached the bench, with bags in his hands and he too looked tired from all his shopping.

He started rummaging threw his bags and got my attention.

He then pulled out a box. I turned and looked and smiled at the elderly man. He held the box in his hand.

I looked at the box kind of wondering what was so important to him.

It was a chocolate candy Easter bunny! Decorated really cute! Then he looked at me and said while pointing at the Easter bunny,

"I remember years ago buying the solid chocolate Easter bunnies, where as there also, seemed to be a more solid understanding of what the Easter celebration was all about.

Now days, most of the Easter bunnies are hollow on the inside. When shopping I feel a hollowness inside of me." I smiled again and replied, "things just aren't like they used to be like at all."

Looking in another direction he pointed his finger and said, "look at that window display over their. Easter eggs, Easter dresses, Easter hats, Easter baskets, Easter flowers, Easter grass, Easter lights, and chocolate everything!

There's more to Easter than hollow chocolate and a hollow perception of the Easter Holiday.

The question is, have we missed the point of Easter and hollowed out it's real meaning?"

I thought a moment and replied, "We should hope not. We should always remember that Easter is a time to celebrate the greatest events this world has ever known.

Did you know that the Easter season is one of the two most important holidays in the Christian calendar, the other being Christmas. These two holidays are like bookends."

"I never thought of that." He said, as he began to rethink what I just said.

I spoke again, "Christmas introduces us to the human life of Jesus Christ and Easter brings together the final purpose of His life on earth." "You are right." He replied. "The cross is the foundation that the Christian faith is built upon. Easter is an encompassing celebration. Easter is a time to acknowledge His great love that he had for all of us.

Most important, Jesus found great love for all of us, as his hands were nailed to the cross for all of us, for our sins."

"That's a very brave statement." He said.

I paused and replied, "I think more so, that Jesus actions of dying on the cross left us with a very brave statement of what great love He had for all of us."

LIVING IN A WORLD OF TRUTH

Every year as Easter approaches, the stores are filled with Easter eggs, jelly beans, chocolate Easter bunnies, and candy in many different varieties.

Easter window clings, figurines of ceramic, cloth, and wooden momentous are pre- maid.

The Easter Lily, and many colorful Easter baskets ranging from small to extra large in size to hold and carry all of our Easter bounty, will soon be surrounded by the Easter green grass.

A little boy just 9 years of age went running to his mother one day as he uttered a hopeful plea.

He began his complaint, "I'm tired of colorful tails and story telling. The Easter bunny never laid Easter eggs only chicken's do.

I don't want you to invent a world for me that I will never see to be true when I get older.

Don't make up a plot that takes wild rollercoaster trips in my mind.

I'm trying to figure out the world so I can make sense of this life we live in.

Half the time I have to have my imagination fill in the gaps of Easter.

I don't want you to take a wash cloth and wipe my face and hands from messy chocolate and say, "this is what Easter is all about." I want stories that are rooted and true to life.

I don't want the story that begins with the magic words, "Once upon a time."

49

The mother understood his plea.

She responded to her son, "We should all be aware that Easter isn't simply a commercial spring festivity about dying eggs and hiding them, or wearing the cutest spring attire.

Easter isn't to be considered an economy booster. Easter is a time to celebrate the greatest events this world has ever known.

Christmas and Easter are like bookends. Christmas introduces us to the human life of Jesus Christ, and Easter brings together the final purpose of his life on earth.

Easter is a time to acknowledge His great love that He had for all of us.

Easter is the Christian observance of the crucifixion of Jesus Christ and his resurrection days latter.

It is one of the oldest observance held within the Christian Church. Easter is held every year at a different times. Anywhere from March 22 to April 25, this special Easter occasion is held."

Many sunrise services are held for people to attend. It's a time to give thanks for all Jesus has done for each and everyone of us."

The little boy was satisfied with the answer his mother gave him.

He smiled and said, "now that sounds like a story to be true." The mother returned a smile and said, "It is true."

The little boy paused and said, "mom, you should hear the story the neighbor boy has about dinosaur pirates in outer space."

The mother replied, "I think I'll pass."

"I think I'll make a plea like you did and want to hear the truth."

Sometimes We Wonder About the World Around Us (May)

Who Am I?

One beautiful sunny day, a minister was going for a leisure walk. He spotted a group of teens sitting in a circle. As he took a closer look, he saw them meditating really hard. Every once in awhile, one teen would write a few words and then went back to that same deep meditating disposition.

The minister respectfully asked what they all were concentrating so hard on. One of the teens replied "Oh, we're doing a paper for the Bible study group that we belong to."

Another teen replied, "It's really as easy question. It didn't take long for me to write my paper."

The minister asked, "What is the question?" The teen replied, "The question is, who am I?"

The minister asked the teens if he could join them. The teens were very excited and wanted him to join them very much.

The teens went to the community center to read their essays, where the minister was also in attendance.

The first teen asked, "Who am I? He then began speaking about how he was a farm person and loved being out in the fields and being around animals.

How he enjoyed being with his friends.

He was a baseball card collector, and traded his cards with others.

To him, that is who he felt he was.

The second teen then read her paper. "I enjoy movies, shopping, dancing, and being with my friends. I am a person who is interested in gardening. I like to go to amusement parks and go on rides. I am a person who likes ice cream treats. I just like to have fun and laugh." To her, that is who she felt she was.

The third teen read his paper. "I am a person who goes to church. I believe in God. I enjoy singing in the choir. I like to play basketball. I like to snowmobile in the winter. I like to fish, swim,

and play my guitar. I like fast food restaurants, and being with my friends." That is who he felt he was.

The fourth teen looked at her sheet and then at the other three teens. A huge smile came to her face, but she paused uneasily in silence. She looked back at her paper and paused again before she said slowly "Who am I?

Again, with a huge smile on her face she said, "Who am I? Me. I'm myself. No other. No duplicate. No clone. God created me, and I'm who He wants me to be. Nothing more. Nothing less. Nothing else."

"That's true for you as well. Be natural. The only way to be somebody is to be yourself."

"Trying to wear another's personality, to look and act like him, is hard at first and becomes impossible later. In the drama of life we are cast in only one role. Yourself. We should play it, not imitate another. I need to learn to be me. No one else is as well qualified as I am."

"Each of us has been uniquely shaped by God's hand. He has formed us exactly to his plan. We don't have to be anybody but ourselves."

"As we walk with Christ, he's in the process of making us more like himself. God created us into who we are.

1 Timothy 4:4 "For every creature of God is good, and nothing to be refused, if it be received with thanksgiving."

If ever questioned who are you? A simple answer, "God's unique creation."

"There's nobody just like you. Never has been, never will be. Only you can be you. Be whom God created you to be. Be yourself, and be the person you hope to be."

Everyone in attendance was amazed. They shook their head as if this was something they never heard before.

Following their speeches, the minister walked over to the four teens and complimented them on the terrific job they had all done.

He then said, "My curiosity makes me wonder about something. Why did you pause and have a bit of a struggle before reading your paper? I thought what you wrote was beautiful, and for the most part, true."

The young teen cleared her throat and replied," "When I heard what the other three wrote about themselves, I became insecure, knowing my paper was written in a different way, and wasn't sure the people would enjoy what I wrote. Or maybe they would think I missed the question altogether. I was filled with fear and lost my confidence for a moment." "In a spark of a second, I regained confidence and then went

forward. Boldly realizing that, that is who I am."

The minister smiled at the teen and raised his voice and replied, "Your paper was written in a different format that's all. You were only expressing yourself in a different manner. It's very evident, you were being whom God created you to be.

Dandelions-The Wonder Of God's Creation

O ne day while driving home from work I just happen to glance over to one of the road sides, to my amazement I saw nothing but dandelions.

Them being of such a bright yellow color they brought on a little cheerfulness within my day.

I then remembered fondly when I was small, I would enjoy running threw the grass barefoot.

I would freely run, eventually, I would raise my hands in the air and catch a breath of some country fresh air.

Then, every once in awhile, I would spot a dandelion on the lawn.

I would stop, stoup down and pick the dandelion.

In time, I had one of my hands full of dandelions.

I would bring them indoors and place them in a glass of water. To me, they were beautiful yellow flowers.

Now, I am older and consider the humble dandelion, a wonder of God's creation.

It begins as a tiny feathery seed that drifts on the wind until it finds a piece of ground and becomes the curse of lawn lovers everywhere.

If left to their own devices, dandelions could completely cover a yard in know time.

I've heard the reason the dandelion is so hardy is because of it's deep taproot, which is twice the height of the plant above ground.

You can try to pull them, but if you leave even a portion of the root, they grow back as strong as ever.

Dandelions have mastered every survival skill including drought. However one thing they haven't mastered is the art of growing in rows.

Years ago, a religion teacher used the dandelion in his classroom as a comparison and example to our faith.

He wanted us to have a better understanding of the word, faith. Holding the bright yellow dandelion in his hand he explained.

"Through His word and sacraments, God causes our faith to grow more robust and sturdy than the dandelions.

He gives us a tough, stubborn faith that weathers any storm and thrives in any condition.

He gives us a blooming faith obvious to anyone who sees it. A faith whose seeds, guided and watered by the spirit, spreads, sprouts, and takes root in people's lives.

That is the kind of faith He gives us in Christ, who endured the cross in faith, to live for us forever."

We now think of the bright yellow dandelion as a wonder of God's creation.

Jesus Is All Powerful

A t different times, within our life time, many of us will find ourselves willing to pay for power.

There are also many different ways that we demonstrate the word "power."

We discover that the fishing boat we have isn't powerful enough to pull a skier. We then buy a boat with a few extra feet added on including a bigger motor. We now have the power to fill our fun filled desires.

We upgrade our computers for more speed memory.

We buy bigger vehicles to carry more stuff. Our inners feel we need heated side mirrors, open sky roof, cruse control, heated seats, and keyless entry to eliminate the keys from being locked inside. We now feel powerful.

We consider power when we buy many things. Yet no matter how much power we may purchase, everything we buy has limited power. Human power is limited.

Doctors can fight sickness and disease with medicine and various procedures, but they cannot ultimately prevent death.

We buy brand-name steel toe boots to prevent injury to our feet at work. Yet Jesus walked many miles to do his work in just a pair of sandals.

The world paints us a picture of power as being of money, muscle, tanks, guns, bombs, strength, and of material items living beyond our means.

Yet man is more powerful when he is in prayer than when he is behind the most powerful guns.

A Christian pictures the cross as being all powerful.

A knowledge specialist will tell you that there is a overwhelming amount of informational literature published for anyone to read.

Yet we discover it is impossible for anyone to read and absorb all the new information discovered yearly.

We need to expect that no matter how hard we try it is impossible to know everything we need to know about some given topics.

Although, there is one area where we have been given everything we need to know.

God has given us everything we need to know for salvation and eternal life.

This informational book is called the Bible. The Bible is a very powerful book from start to finish.

The Bible teaches us that Jesus was born in an obscure village. He worked in a carpenter shop until he was thirty.

He continually shared his God-given gifts with the world around him unselfishly.

He became a itinerant preacher.

Some of the amazing truth's are that Jesus never held an office. He never had a family or owned a house. He didn't go to college. He had no credentials but himself.

He did however, give an out-pour of His love. That love given to mankind was given to us without limit. He engraved each and everyone of us on the palm of His hands with the mark of nails.

Many centuries have come and gone.

Today he is still the strong figure of the human race.

All the armies that ever marched to protect you and I. All the navies that went to sea that ever sailed. All the air force that protected us from above. All the marines that submerged to the depths of the waters, have not effected the life of man on this earth as much as what Jesus has done for us.

Jesus is all-powerful, and he wants us to trust in him even when we don't understand his ways. He wants us to believe that He is all-powerful to work in our present situations.

Today, He is the central figure because He remains all-powerful. Luke 1:37 "For with God nothing shall be impossible."

Would You Have Noticed?

If a Bible were found in an old house, in an attic, in a dusty cardboard box.

Would you notice that all along, that I, "the Bible", was surrounded by darkness, crawly insects, and many cobwebs?

Would you pick me up and gently wipe me off or would you leave me dusty and pass me on by?

Would you look at me and say, "You look mighty lonely, would you like to be mine? I've never known you to fail mankind."

Would you notice that I was unpleasantly stored in a place of darkness with no one to hold me, read me, or share my words to others?

Would you notice that God is the Author of me, the Bible, a book that's forever selling?

Would you notice that all my stories compiled was never written or ever started with, "once upon a time?"

Would you notice by opening me up and by reading me daily that I was well worth your time?

Would you notice that I was a book that never became outdated?

Would you notice that I was a book for all ages.

Would you notice that within time, any darkness within your soul was slowly leaving?

Would you notice that the bright light within my words was only to be found?

Would you notice that I was of complete truth, obedience, and a guide for all, in times of need?

Would you notice that my written words were never meant to hurt you. They were only there to help you, encourage you, and heal your biggest wound.

Would you notice that the words written are our greatest source of comfort when you are hurt, worried, or frightened.

Would you notice that my words penetrated and softly blanketed your heart and soul.

Would you notice that God is all powerful with comfort no human can ever match.

Would you notice that by sending God's message to others, that by doing so others would be finding the truth about salvation.

Would you notice and be amazed if someone said, "I just learned about a man named Jesus. I did not know him until I met you."

"Would you notice that all along telling others about the Bible has been and will always be our work in the world."

"Would you have noticed?"

I Was Just Wondering

From day to day we all live in a day of wonder. We all wonder about something.

We wonder what's in the inside of Timmy's Birthday present.

We wonder how much the mechanic is going to charge for overhauling our motor in our car.

We wonder when our children are going to get married.

We wonder what movie is going to being playing next at the movie theater.

We wonder what are next raise is going to be like, if any?

We wonder what the next song is going to be first on the charts. We wonder what technology is going to come up with next.

We wonder about the lump on our leg.

We wonder what a new recipe we are trying is going to taste like. We all wonder about many things through-out the day and everyday. One day a young adult girl was sitting next to an elderly lady.

The girl was wondering.

She turned to the elderly lady and asked, "when you were in school what not so smart of things did you do?"

The elderly lady chuckled. Her face turned beet red.

She then put her hand over her mouth in embarrassment and replied, "I remember when I was in the third grade in school. I told my teacher I wasn't going to come to school anymore."

The teacher asked me, "Why aren't you going to come to school anymore?"

I told her, "I knew all my A, B, C's and I knew my 1,2, 3's and could count all the way to 100."

I told her, "I knew how to add and subtract."

I told her, "I knew all the names of my color crayons in my crayon box."

The girl was curious, "what happened then?"

The elderly lady laughed again, and said, "The teacher told me to tell my parents that I was not going to come to school anymore because I thought I was smart enough and didn't need to attend school any longer."

The next morning came. I said to my dad, "I'm not going to school because, I'm smart enough and don't need to go to school."

I was planning to go to Uncle Jerry's house to play with his cat and dog.

My dad said, "no, your not. If you don't want to go to school I will put you to work because that's what people do when they are out of school, they work for a living."

"That wasn't any fun at all." I said. The next day my dad tried to wake me.

I turned to him and said, "I don't want to go to school because I don't feel good."

He went to the medicine cabinet and got some not so good tasting medicine for my tummy. I had to take the medicine or it would look like I wasn't sick.

The medicine was horrible. My dad made me stay in bed. I couldn't watch T.V. and I was bored to death.

The next day came, my dad came to my bedside and asked, "Are you going to go to school today?"

I turned to him with a smile and said, "yes, Dad I'm going to school today. I need to learn how to become a better student."

Summertime, A Time Of Learning And Discovery (June)

Learning And Discovering

Some of us may remember, when we were small children, how we enjoyed and found is a challenge to climb as high as we possibly could in a tree.

The strategy while climbing up in the tree was to prevent falling out of the tree.

Yet, being convinced we could get to the highest part of that tree, we continued in determination.

We grabbed onto the limb and pulled with all our might, stretching and gripping our hands around the tree branches that surrounded us, only wanting to go forward.

Our feet played an important part in our ever-forward motion.

Our legs were entangled around the limb of the tree, supporting our internal fears. We wanted to see how high we could get.

It was a true experience of going beyond our everyday natural abilities.

It was a feeling of freedom. Examining our every move as we went forward was a challenge. Should we take that next step, grasp on, and go forward? How much more will this limb support without breaking off from the tree?

We all know there are consequences when climbing trees, such as falling flat on our faces, possible injury, and "ouch that hurt!"

Climbing the tree and returning back down is just as challenging. We are much relieved when we are back down, and can announce that we are at ground level and safe.

Zaccheus, the wee little man, had different intentions for climbing a tree. Jesus was surrounded by people, and since Zaccheus was a wee little man, he couldn't see Jesus. He wanted to see what Jesus was like.

Zaccheus, with much energy, ran ahead and climbed a sycamore tree which was along Jesus route, in order to see him.

When Jesus reached the spot, he looked up and said unto him, Luke 19:5-6 "Zaccheus, make haste, and come down; for to day I must abide at thy house." And he made haste, and came down, and received him joyfully.

Isn't it amazing how we all have different reasons for what we do in life to fulfill our needs?

Zaccheus not only went to great length and measure to climb the sycamore tree to see Jesus, but the wee little man learned much more. He examined his way in life and chose to follow Jesus' ways.

The wee little man was searched out by Jesus, and he was saved by Jesus.

The wee little man discovered that Jesus saved him, for he was lost.

God Finishes What He Starts

A father noticed that his teenage son had an interest in looking up into the sky at night, asking questions about the stars and the moon.

The father decided one day that he was going to buy his son a telescope so he could learn more.

The son received his telescope and was very excited. He enjoyed what he saw and learned something new every day when he peered through his telescope.

The father walked up to his son one night and asked, "Is your telescope teaching you anything in particular?"

The son backed up from his telescope with a questionable look on his face and replied, "I'm very fascinated with my telescope and all that I see at a distance. One thing that puzzles me is that God made the sun, moon, earth, stars, Jupiter, Mars and all the other planets in just one week.

"Yet, Jesus is working on each and every one of us every day being whom he's created us to be. Just think how loving and patient he must be. When I stumble and when I fall I should have a sign upon my heart that says "God isn't finished with me yet; he's still working on me."

The father, putting his hand on his son's shoulder said, "God's the potter and you're the clay. He's molding you into what you should be according to the master hand. God always finishes what he starts. Unlike us, God never carries over items on his "To-do" list. He has a blueprint for your life spread before him. The travel map is drawn up, and he knows the direction and miles between you and him. He won't stop until he's done. He has the ultimate plan, to make you more like Jesus."

Bringing The Best To Others In Their Time Of Need

One beautiful Saturday afternoon a mother and her 14 year old son sat in their porch swing swinging back and forth.

Every once in awhile a gentle breeze would pass through leaving the air filled with a fresh scent of lilac.

The mother glanced at her son and noticed that his eyes were starring at a air plane that just passed over. He quickly turned his head, he saw a bird nest up in a tree. He was amused by the birds as they chirped.

She then observed that his hands and arms were in full motion swaying in all directions. His legs swung back and forth nervously.

The mother chuckled and said, "you're such a busy boy." The son giggled and replied, "I'm just making sure all my body parts are working today."

The mother raised her eye brows and said to her son, "I have something I would like to teach you that I was taught.

I have a question for you. I want you to give me the best answer that you can possibly give me. I will let you know when you find the answer I'm looking for."

The son agreed.

The mother said to her son, "What is the most important part of your body to others in their time of need?"

Thinking very hard he blurted out, "I think the most important part of my body to others in their time of need are my ears. We need to listen to others"

The mother said, "no, that's not the most important body part to others because many people are deaf. You keep on thinking and I will ask you again soon."

Several days passed. She asked her son again. This time he thought the most important body part was his sight. "It's important that everybody can see, it must be our sight. "It's important that everybody can see, it must be our eyes." He said.

She looked at her son and replied, "you're getting smarter, but the answer is not correct. There are many people who are blind."

The son looked down at his feet. In a split second he blurted out, "It must be our feet!"

The mother said, "no, many people travel by wheel chair without difficulty."

A few days went by and the son came up to his mothers side while she sat embroidering.

The boy took a deep breath and said, "mother, it's got to be our hands."

The mother replied, "no, it's not our hands. Although our hands help others everyday. There are many people who have lost their hands due to accidents."

The mother saw confusion in her son's face and reassured her son that the question was very important. "When you find the correct answer, it'll show that you have really lived within your life." She said. The mother looked at her son and reassured him and said, "For every body part you gave me in the past, I have told you why you were

incorrect. Trust me, today you will find your answer."

The mother told her son that she was going to the funeral home. A close friend of hers had died in a sudden car accident. She wanted him to come along.

The son agreed.

The son sat on a chair and watched many people come and go.

He observed people of all ages, hugging, comforting, and shaking hands.

Tears were coming from everybody.

In a split second, he thought he had his answer.

He approached his mother and whispered in her ear. "The most important body part to others in their time of need has to be our shoulder."

The mother smiled at her son and said, "you found the right answer. Our shoulder help others in their time of need. People of all walks of life become fail and weak. We sometimes feel like were going to crumble. The fountain of tears flow without end leaving us lifeless and in total awe. Everybody needs a shoulder to cry on sometime within our day or life. I only hope that you have a shoulder to cry on when you need it." The son realized that the most important body part was of great need. It wasn't considered selfish. It was considered an extension of our

human love to one another.

To uplift, to strengthen, and to bring compassion into the depths of another person's soul. Our shoulder can be shared with many, and is considered our jumper cables to rejuvenating mankind.

Our true example was Jesus, he was sympathetic and compassionate to the pain and needs of others.

A Special Father's Day Gift

A little boy, just 8 years of age, decided he wanted to give his father something really special for Father's Day.

First, he decided he wanted to buy the gift with his own money.

Then, he decided, it would have to be something fun the two could do together, as father and son.

Finally, he decided that he wanted the gift to bring a memory to his father on his special day.

The little boy managed to come up with an idea and was very excited.

He couldn't wait to present his gift to his father on Father's Day.

The special day came and the little boy, with a beaming look on his face, went running up to his father with his special gift.

The father could see the excitement in his son's face, and he, too, became just as excited as his son.

The father exclaimed very proudly, "what a perfect gift you chose for me on Father's Day!"

It was a kite the two could fly together.

It was a bright and colorful kit that could only bring a smile to your face when you saw it.

The father went outside and looked up into the sky.

He took his son by the hand and the two walked out to a spacious bare field.

It was a fine day to go kite-flying.

The wind was brisk and billowy clouds were blowing across the sky.

The kite went up, until it was entirely hidden by the clouds. "What are you doing? The boy asked his father."

"I'm flying a kite," the father replied.

The little boy was squinting his eyes. He could no longer see the kite. He became restless.

"I can't see the kite!" he exclaimed.

The father with a reassuring voice said, "I can't see the kite either, but every once in awhile, I feel a tug, so I know for sure that the kite is up there."

The father put the kite string in between two of his son's fingers. The little boy still couldn't see the kite, but he felt a tug. The tug startled the little boy, as his eyes lit up and a smile came to his face.

The father looked at his son and said, "I'm very happy with your gift of a kite, given to me, on Father's Day, but most importantly, I am happy with the thought of us being together, flying the kite and generating memories."

"If you'll let me, I have just one thing I want to teach you about kite flying. I also want you to remember what I taught you forever."

The little boy shook his head and promised that he would remember.

The father looked up into the sky and the little boy followed with his head, moving it in the same direction. The father took his pointer finger and pointed at the kite that neither one of them could see.

"The kite you gave me is up there, however, you just can't see it. God is the same way. He's up there, but you can't see Him.

The most important thing is to find Him for yourself. You, too, will know by the wonderful, warm tug on your heartstring, that He is there, for sure, for you, at all times and in all circumstances."

The little boy smiled and replied, "Happy Father's Day. I really think this memory is going to last a lifetime."

God Heals Our Hurts

There is not one person who lives a carefree life. We all live with physical, emotional distress, loss and heart ache.

We are all in the same boat together trying to stay afloat. None of us have palm branches fanning us while were being served grapes to eat in the comfort of a soft cushy high back chair in our boat.

We all try to smile between disasters in finding splashes of joy. It's the surviving in the cesspool and eventually climbing out that takes the ability to deal with pain and grief.

The waves splash into our boat causing us to be pushed backwards. We go this way and that way. The waves cause are boat to go up and down in motion.

Then finally we discover we have a hole in our boat and all we can do is sink.

Nothing comes into our lives by accident; no matter how bad it makes you feel, it didn't come to stay but to pass.

The hard part is dealing with being alive while waiting for whatever it is to pass.

When we are over-loaded and capsized with pain and grief sometimes are thoughts are the feeling of sinking to the lowest level imaginable.

Our first discovery maybe that our tears have a language all of their won.

In some mysterious way, our complex inner communication system knows when to admit it's verbal limitations… and the tears come.

Our mind is blank and were left without expression.

Sometimes we may even think, which is worse, emotional or physical pain?

Like most of us, we have faced both kinds: crushing physical pain with no position in which we can get comfortable; crushing heartache in which our head spins with grief and we can't stop the tears.

As Proverbs says, "Heartache crushes the spirit."

You can almost distract yourself from physical pain. But inside suffering, that's another matter. It can only be known, really know, by God.

The second discovery maybe, you can't put mental anguish or heartache behind you. Those hurts create an emptiness that refuses to be pushed out or crowed out of your thoughts. The situation bites, it gnaws, it grinds away at your spirit.

It's most convincing that emotional pain is much worse than physical pain.

We should also be convinced that emotional pain does something to our heart that physical pain often can't.

The third discovery maybe, our inner anguish melts the heart, making our soul pliable and bendable. That's because we can't drive it from our thoughts, it forces us to embrace God out of desperate, urgent need.

God is never closer than when your hurting inside.

Many prayers are answered as God gently touches our hurts and in time makes us whole again.

OUR WORLD CONSISTS OF MANY
GOOD THINGS BUT, SETTING
A GOOD EXAMPLE OUTLIVES
THEM ALL (JULY)

Instilling Our Values And Morals

On The 4th Of July

E very year, friends and family gather around and take the time to celebrate the true purpose and tradition of Independence Day, also known as the Fourth of July.

The children run and play as we partake in barbeques, picnics, reminiscing, and later on the fireworks displays bring people of all ages flocking to parks and lakefronts in many communities.

Friends and family watch the unfolding fireworks show from a blanket, lawn chair, or bleacher sending many oohs and aahs of appreciation as a burst of rockets follows a towering Roman candle. The sky is lit up with multiple explosions of many colored starbursts, pinwheels, and sizzling comet tails.

Everything breaks loose with a spectacular grad finale, with a sky full of reds, greens, blues, and gold's on behalf of this special occasion. It's also a day to be instilling the values and morals of our Christian heritage in the minds and hearts of others, while we pay homage to our country.

It should be emphasized that this great nation was built on godly principles and the freedom to worship God as our forefathers did.

This country was founded by great people. They stood for what they knew was right. They didn't ignore, or take for granted God's handiwork, or turn their heads to look the other way.

The dreams of our forefathers were built with blood and tears. Their boldness meant to keep this country standing strong throughout the many years.

The flag we own is proudly flown to show respect and how much we care.

The bright stars and the many stripes, spell freedom. God, above, has brought this day to light, with just a stroke of liberty and a touch of his great hand. He gave democracy to us and helped this country stand. Placing your hand on your heart as you turn to face the flag for battles that were fought, be filled with pride for those who died and

freedoms that were bought.

Pause for a moment as you watch the fireworks bright dazzling display. Remember God is watching and guiding us every step of the way.

Those of us a distance do what we can to support the troops. We drive around with our "Support the Troops" stickers on our cars, posters, logos, benefits, and praying fervently for their safety and success. That's why we take the time to paint the sky with fireworks on the Fourth of July.

God's Ways Are Better Than Our Ways

One day in a shopping mall two elderly ladies sat besides each other on a bench.

They were both people watching and resting for a moment.

They both noticed some shoppers walked really fast and some dwindled looking in all directions. Some were window shoppers and some held and examined every pair of shoes on display.

Some were chewing gum nervously and the next person was content with a smile on their face.

One shopper was in a wheel chair and the next walked with a cane.

A teenager walked by with high heels that went clickety- click and another one walked by with a stroller filled with children.

One shopper had many bags and the next shopper carried one tiny box.

Each shopper had their own unique look about how they shopped within their day.

One of the elderly ladies started to laugh and said, "my hair is starting to thin-out and turn silver. I know I have many years behind me and just a few ahead of me.

I reckon within a short time this is all I will be able to do is sit and people watch. I don't get around like I used too. I have somewhat of a limp and arthritis is taking it's toll."

The other elderly lady responded by saying, "I've traveled and done many things in life myself. I too, am slowing up.

I just hope when my traveling days have come to a stationary position of a recliner that there'll be no thought of any unkind words I've said that left a trail of sorrow of a memory of a bitter scene I have created.

I don't want to sit regretting what I could have, should have done with my bygone yesterday."

The other elderly lady softly replied, "we all know, we can't stop the hands of time. There is no fortune teller or crystal ball that will ever be able to determine the future ahead of any given person, today or tomorrow.

There is one thing that I do know for sure. If we could see the end of our life from the beginning, we would choose no other way than which God has chosen for us. God's ways are always better than our ways."

A Special Teacher

Dedicated in Honor
(To: Robert D. Henning of Hutchinson, MN)
(My English Teacher for 35 years at Lester Prairie Public School.
Recently Retired)

We all know, that we have to go to elementary and high school for learning purposes. We all, within our 12 years of school have found a class or a teacher we simply enjoyed or easily learned from over the years.

When we find enjoyment within the school system, we then become more interested in hanging around.

With a piece of paper on my desk in high school and a pen in my hand, the words ran threw me like running water. To me, this was fun and sometimes a bit of a challenge, but I simply enjoyed what I was doing.

As I sit and write today, a reflection from yesterday appear however, much stronger and in a different light.

I'm not in school any longer, that day is in the past. I have no teacher to watch over me and direct me every step of the way, I'm on my own. I have no teacher that gives me a dead-line for my work to be completed. I'm responsible for my own dead-line and for what I choose to write.

As I sit and write, you must realize that all that was learned and taught is compiled together and is now considered knowledge. What I do with that knowledge is totally up to me.

A teacher is not only a teacher, he/she teaches his/her students that they will become the next generation of teachers.

A teachers teaching skills will ultimately show down the road how well he/she taught his/her/students. In time there will be a reflection down the road of your teachers teaching skills taught to others by you. You were once the student, you now become the teacher of what you were taught.

I believe God works threw others to bring the best to others in the spirit of joyfulness and that special joy is called, "a gift."

One of the amazing attributes is, my teacher will always consider me his student, while I will always consider him my teacher no matter what each one of us does in life.

As I end my story, I've searched over and over again and I can't find the right words to describe what I was taught and what I obtained over the years by my teachers classroom skills, nor all his acts of kindness. My Webster Dictionary says, "neither can I!"

What can a person write or say when you can't comprehend the excellence of ones teachings?

The many stories written will then speak for themselves and live on in the heart and soul of many!

"Our world consists of many good things but setting a good example out lives them all!"

THE ELOQUENCE OF HIS EXAMPLE

There was an elderly man by the name of John. He came into a community uneducated and poor. A Minister directed him to a Industrial steel company.

He was taught his job position by upper management. He diligently worked many long hours. By the end of the day he was dirty from head to toe. You could only see the whites of his eyes.

He talked very little. However, he wore the most cheerful smile. His clothes were tattered. His shoes had holes that were badly worn,

they slipped up and down his heels as he walked.

John carried with him every day to work a pocket hand-sized Bible. He would often show employees a Bible verse when they were in need of encouragement.

One day John didn't show up for work. Employee's noticed a note was put up on the bulletin board, saying he had passed away from a massive heart attack. The employees were heart-broken from the news. John's two sons lived at a distance. They received the news of the death of their father and came home right away to make arrangements. There were many beautiful plants and flowers that surrounded the casket. The two sons sat together and starred at their father who was

all they had left.

Everything was a blur to them. All they could see was the life of a simple man. One of the son's turned to view behind them. All the people who had come to show their respect to their father.

John's supervisor, Jeff sat with the two sons. He comforted them in their time of sorrow.

Jeff whispered to the sons, "as you can see your father touched the hearts of many."

The Minister walked up to the pulpit and said, "you'll never know when your going to be taught a lesson in life."

The crowd of people stirred in their pews. The Minister began slowly speaking. "This man came to this church one day. I never saw him before or knew of him. I found him in prayer. I asked him if there was some- thing I could do for him." He smile and replied, "I need job and a black book."

I managed to piece together what he was saying for his English was poor. I got him a pocket hand -sized Bible. I wrote 10 words on the front page of his Bible.

I walked him outside and pointed to the Industrial steel building. I told him to go there and ask for top management. He was to open his Bible and show them what I wrote.

The Minister said. "there is only one thing that makes a dream impossible to achieve: the fear of failure." "This man, had no sign of thinking, he was going to fail. He just wanted a job. What he did not lack was faith."

John opened his Bible to the front page, Jeff read what was written.

This is what I wrote the Minister said,

"Never look down on any-body unless you're helping them up." Jeff understood that John was struggling in life and gave him a job.

He also trained him in. John taught others all they needed to know about faith and hard working by the simple eloquence of his example.

The Minister looked at the casket slowly turning his head viewing the people in the church.

The Minister said. "This man may have been known to be uneducated and poor. Amazingly, if we search within, he set an example. He was authentic. He enveloped each and everyone of you with his heart of love. He touched your soul beyond what education could ever teach.

"In life, people will not always remember what you said. People will not always remember to the fullest what you did. However, people will always remember how you made them feel. Look around. His simple eloquence of his example surrounds you all here today."

A Heart Broken Tragedy, In Time,

Reaches Out To Others

One day in a nursing home facility, an elderly lady by the name of Jenny, with gray naturally wave, fluffy hair, sat content in an old wooden rocker.

Jenny was blessed with a beautiful skin tone with a few wrinkles around her deep sky blue eyes.

Jenny had the disposition of a well mannered secretary. Her smile was golden which was attached to her positive well spoken words she extended to others. With every rock of the rocking chair her eyes circled around the solarium room, at the other residents.

Every once in a while she'd glanced out a big picture window, she was watching the traffic at a highway near by. Her legs were crossed and her hands laid peacefully in her lap. Her hands were soft and her finger nails were manicured and had the look of the hands of those seen in a glamour or some type of beauty magazine.

A staff person sat next to Jenny one day. The staff person received word that Jenny would be leaving soon, to live in another facility closer to her family.

The staff person became curious. She asked, "Jenny how many children do you have?"

Jenny with out a slur of her words said, "I have four children. Two boys and two girls. My first son is a Dentist. My second son was in college and was taken from me. My third, a daughter is a Nurse. My fourth, a daughter, is a sales clerk."

The staff person was filled with curiosity and questioned Jenny.

"I heard you say that your second child was taken from you, how did this happen?"

Jenny spoke freely without hesitation. "My second son was in college. He was a very smart student. The other students became jealous of him at times, because he received good grades.

One night a group of his college students decided they wanted to go bar hopping. My son wasn't much of a drinker, if any.

The group became tired of seeing him take little sips. This wasn't considered party time for them at all.

The group decided to throw some money together and purchase themselves a bottle of whiskey.

To the country roads they all went. My son became a part of a group that was out of control.

They offered my son whiskey straight from the bottle. He took one sip. The sip was something the group was tired of seeing. They yelled at him, "drink more!" He refused.

They became angry and grabbed him and poured the whiskey forcibly down his throat. He chocked on the whiskey and died that evening."

The staff lady questioned, "Was their an investigation? Were their any arrests? Did you retain an Attorney?"

Jenny said, "No. My health couldn't take anymore and I decided to let God handle it all on his own."

The staff lady said with a sigh, "According to the Bible that is what were suppose to do. Were suppose to extend our problems into the hands of God."

Jenny continued, "The person responsible was happy he wasn't charged. The discovery was, he began to drink more to cover up his pain inside of him. I did tell him one time that, God saw all that he did when he took my son away from me, that was all that mattered.

The last we heard was that the responsible college student lost one of his eyes."

He returned back to me one day and said, "drinking wasn't a part of his life anymore."

He became a guest speaker and told others about what drinking can do to family and friends if, not watching intake while drinking."

Jenny felt blessed by God that others were touched and learning from this tragedy.

Our Surroundings Bring On
A New Perspective
(August)

The Rocker

One day while in a furniture store a pregnant mother was looking at all the different styles of rocking chairs. She wanted to purchase one but was uncertain as to which one she wanted. Her baby was soon to be born. She wanted something that would be comfortable, while she held her new baby in her arms and rocked him/her to sleep.

The store owner walked over and asked the mother if she needed help selecting a rocking chair. The pregnant mother sighed and said, "yes, I do. I don't know which rocking chair will be the best for fulfilling my babies needs."

The store owner replied, "I know my mother rocked me. I was rocked in a unfinished rocker. It was their first exciting piece of furniture they purchased when I was born. My mother hummed many songs into me as we clung to each other."

The pregnant mother chuckled and said, "My mother always said rocking a child raised the IQs of a child.

She said it was important to hold, hug and touch a child while you rocked them to sleep or soothed them."

The store owner said, "I believe rocking is a part of us all. It's how we stayed alive in our mother for nine months."

The mother thought a moment and said, "If you really think about it the story of Noah's family in the flood. They rocked and rocked, 40 days and 40 nights. They were in the midst of a storm. Inside they rocked back and forth while being content of the outside world, the wind, the rain, and the danger."

The store owner said, "Moses, He led Israel to a promised land.

He was rocked in a basket, in water filled with bulrushes."

The mother walked over to a rocker and sat in it. She closed her eyes, with her arms relaxing on the arms of the chair and back and forth she rocked.

Opening her eyes, she said, "this chair has a squeak."

Store owner replied, "most wooden rockers have music with them. They squeak."

Going to the next rocker. It looked cozy.

She sat in it and gave a big sigh. "This chair is the perfect chair. I want to purchase this one."

The store owner gave a smile and said, "I have three rocking chairs at home and all three of them rock differently. They all serve the same purpose, they rocked and soothed my children to sleep.

One rocker was unfinished, the second rocker had a squeak and the last rocker was soft and fluffy when you sat in it and rocked."

The mother smiled and said, "This rocker was different when I sat in it. I knew right away I wanted this one."

The store owner questioned, "why do you like that rocker?"

The mother replied, "I liked that rocker the most because it was comfortable, it soothed me while I rocked and most of all, I felt held when I was rocking. I felt like God had his arms around me in every motion. He was gently comforting me. He was taking the discontentment in my life and soothing my thoughts and bringing a renewal to my walk in life."

Being Blessed

A person was looking at the Sunday Paper one day, scanning over some of the stories to see what was happening in other parts of the world.

Sometimes you'll find stories of unfortunate homicides, medical stories, abduction stories, people winning awards, government issues, runaways, inflation, sports, pollution, discoveries, people of talent, and many more interesting topics.

Flipping the page, most often we are curious about the weather. We search for the area we live in and see what the temperature is going to be like. We wonder if it's going to rain, snow, sleet, be windy, cloudy, warm, hot, or if the sun is going to come out and be a wonderful day. Turning the page were always amused with cartoons, word search, crossword puzzles, or some type of trivia.

Slam dunk, right in front of us we see the word, "horoscope."

Most of us give a little chuckle in wonder how our day is going to be. Were really excited when we read were in for prosperity, career change, great awards, travel at a distance expected, unexpected romance, numbers- 2,7,9,11,& 23, are your winning numbers. We become infatuated by the horoscope readings. Everyone has a special reading for their specific birthday. Only to find none of what is written happens realistically.

Now days you can read your horoscope daily, tomorrow, weekly, monthly, or yearly.

We can read about our compatibility, to date, or to marry. How our life style is for whatever given day. Our career, wealth, and our health. To find none of what is written happens realistically.

Another person walking by questioned the person reading the Sunday paper, and asked, "my Birthday's in July. How lucky am I going to be today?"

Another person interrupted the conversation and said to both of them, "The word, "lucky" is not considered the right terminology to be used in the Christian vocabulary at times. Being blessed is."

One of them replied, "Isn't lucky being lucky? Doesn't it mean things that seem to happen to a person by chance, good or bad. To have good fortune. He is lucky at winning. A lucky rabbit's foot. A lucky horse shoe. He was lucky at the casino or community drawing?"

The person gave a smile and responded, "None of us were born to revolve around a horoscope, telling us or controlling our everyday destiny. Were ticking by the hands of God's time, not our own thoughts or time.

Each and everyone of us are being blessed everyday somehow or somewhere. Anything that happens to us is considered a Blessing from God, not being considered lucky.

A blessing means to make holy. To ask God's favor for. The Minister blessed the congregation. He didn't say, "I want you to be lucky today. He blessed us."

It means to bring happiness or good fortune to. God bless you. To praise or glorify. In the summer time rain would be a blessing. A new born baby. A marriage. A successful surgery. Anything that brings joy or comfort is a blessing to us."

The person holding the Sunday paper started to read a couple of the horoscopes only to find themselves laughing at their horoscope for that day.

Reading on, she stopped and said in blunt words, "Oh my God, get this. This horoscope says, "a new cycle of blessings is on it's way." It didn't say, a new cycle of luck is on it's way."

This statement only proves a horoscope reading can not or will never predict the future for any person, today, tomorrow, next month, or yearly. God is the only one that will be in complete control of each and everyone of us daily and everyday."

LIVING IN A FAST PACED WORLD

Dedicated in Honor
To: Andrew Meuleners of Winsted, MN
(Managing Edition of the Herald Journal in Winsted, MN)

We live our daily lives at such a fast pace, that some of us would feel insulted if another person were to tell us to slow down.

We skim through the daily paper, magazines and books reading a few words and then skipping over to another article.

We take our remotes and channel surf programs on the television trying to find an appropriate show for our family to watch. We find ourselves only listening to little bits of opinions on the nightly news.

We dash to a fast-food restaurant to pick up our order to eat on our way to our next appointment.

Were moving along at such a fast pace, in some what of a whirl wind stage going from base to base. Our people ideas and experiences never really penetrate deep within us, there just surface thoughts.

Our children make a plea for us to play with them and our response is, "I'm busy or latter."

To sit down with our teenagers is next to impossible because most often there on their own run to be with friends or activities they like to do.

We see people we know on the street or in the stores, we wave or smile to them because we don't have time, were off on the run.

The elderly are put on the back burner of our thoughts because there slower paced.

We live with high blood pressure, anxiety, and stress filled nauseating stomachs.

We speed on the highways, only to find ourselves receiving a high priced speeding ticket. We sigh when the officer tells us, "my job is to make you and others safe while driving on the highways."

The real question lies within each and everyone of us, "what's the hurry all about?"

When were in a hurry were more reluctant to making mistakes or over looking something of importance. Our communication skills are cut in half. Others think of us as having selective hearing.

We need to prioritize and make those closest to us matter in this responsible world we live in.

We need to shut ourselves off from the non important issues. Finding time to relax in a game of cards or a board game with friends and family brings us to a more neutral position.

In time, we realize that running here and running there senselessly gets us no where. We need to set aside those special moments and have a relationship that creates a fresh breeze that enters the heart and soul that calms and refreshes us.

Recharging Ourselves

Dedicated in Honor
(To: Troy Feltmann of Lester Prairie, Mn)
(Sign Dept. Manager of the Herald Journal in Winsted, Mn.)

In today's world, were all shifting gears from one task to the next. Some of us live from day to day with a pen in one hand and a post-it note pad in the other hand. We realize we have a overwhelming to-do

list that can't possible be mastered.

Our E-mail messages travel down the front of our computer which are beyond comprehension.

Our answering machines are filled with people wanting return calls A.S.A.P.

Our cell phone stores messages to be returned and text messages that need attention immediately.

Our caller-I-Dee presents us with telephone numbers galore from telemarketers, friends, and family wanting to talk to us.

The mail we receive starts to form a heaping pile, we sigh, at our own bills that we see.

Our door bell rings in wonder who is on the other side, needing someone to talk too, within our household.

It's hard to give permission to ourselves to take a break or rest for a moment.

It somehow reminds us of a car battery. If we leave a vehicle door open to long or perhaps we leave our interior light on to long, it will drain the battery.

We then need jumper cables to recharge, to get our vehicle running again.

We too, must be replenished with sleep, food, rest, and relaxation. If we don't, before to long our energy is consumed. We are emotionally, physically, mentally drained and considered dead on our feet.

Our thinking becomes somewhat of a blur. Our vision questions, "did I just see what I just saw?"

Our body aches, with no position to comfort us or our pain. Our responses to others becomes negative and short sentenced.

We are simply exhausted in all areas. We all need to be wise to take short breaks now and then through-out our day.

Take a vacation at a distance. Go for regular walks, exercise, eat healthy foods, receive spiritual nourishment, and close our door to get plenty of sleep at night, this will recharge ourselves again. Isaiah 40:31 "But they that wait upon the Lord shall renew their strength: they shall mount up with wings as eagles: they shall run, and not be weary: and they shall walk, and not faint."

Living a well balanced life will help each and everyone of us maintain our energy supply and will enable us to be more productive and a much more happier and content person.

Follow Me

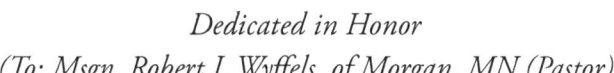

Dedicated in Honor
(To: Msgn. Robert J. Wyffels, of Morgan, MN (Pastor)

This time of the year, there are many people of all ages who wear sandals. There are also many different types of sandals we can purchase at the stores. Generally most of us are wanting something comfortable on our feet.

For those of you who have worn sandals, most likely your feet weren't any different than the next person's feet by the end of the day, they became dirty while wearing the sandals.

The human side and the reality of Jesus wasn't any different. In his many walks his feet resembled ours, they too, became dirty.

Jesus walked many dusty winding gravel roads. He was on a two word mission. Those two simple words are still within our everyday mission. All Jesus said was, "follow me." And they believed him. So, in faith people gave their lives to him. Some put down their nets and followed this sandaled Jewish man.

Thinking about it, this would have been the birthplace of a way of life, of a reality that would change the world forever.

Everywhere he went he said, "Follow me." Eventually he had a band of followers. People responded to him in various ways. Most became intrigued by his healings and miracles.

They started attaching themselves to him. They believed, listened, obeyed, questioned, talked with, and learned from him. This proved to be a thrilling adventure. They saw and witnessed Jesus' great unbelievable works. They captured the miracles no other human could do.

The followers then told others. They just had to tell others about this Jesus. The group of followers in time, became a crowd of followers.

One day Jesus walked step by step in his sandals back to town.

Jesus stopped to heal the sick, touch the blind and brought dignity to the helpless.

There was something different about this Jesus. His teachings, actions, conversations were powerful.

In time people gathered around him to listen to him, to be with him and see what he was going to do next.

Jesus walked as a human among the humans. Jesus taught like no one ever had. Some of his teachings were razor sharp with truth. He cast out his words like fishing line and permanently touched people's souls. He laid down his own net and saved the souls of many.

Eventually, a church was formed to help others follow Jesus. It was a gathering place. A place to be nourished, to be taught, and to reach out to others.

We live in a messed up world, not one of us being better than another.

Were people today, still helping and serving people just like Jesus did. In reality Jesus humbly put his voice, hands, and feet into motion and set a miraculous example.

When you think about all of this, the simple truth is:

"The world will always be in better shape when someone leads the way in forward motion. Instead of saying,"not me!" Leadership is a position not all can do but, it is a job most needed, to direct people in the right direction.

Yes, Jesus led the way by saying,"Follow me." Those two simple words still live on in today's world.

Many souls have been blessed with that u-turn in life. They simply acknowledged those two little words, "Follow me," and they were redirected to a better way of living.

WE LIVE IN A WORLD OF VALUABLE LESSONS (SEPTEMBER)

Children Teach Valuable Lessons

The word "teacher" if you define that word you will be amazed to find that we are all a teacher in life.

We all teach something to someone everyday regardless of our age or our occupation.

Although, little children are the best teachers in the world. They begin teaching at such a young age.

They teach young women to be mothers and young men to be fathers. They become so skilled at it they don't stop their, for then they teach older men and women how to be grandparents.

They teach mom's to be cooks, house cleaners, to focus their attention in all directions, to be nurse's and to be compassionate. They teach dad's to be protectors, mechanics, and to be strong for their family.

They teach brothers and sisters how to share toys, rooms, and their favorite treat.

Children teach the world how to love, hug, laugh, and embrace. They teach us how to look past a person's skin color and to focus on the heart.

They teach us to look beyond another ones faults and to keep peace and to respectfully go forward.

Children keep us honest and to keep our promises because they never let us forget the ones we made to them.

They even teach us to become scientists and professors by asking continuously "why?, how come?, where?, when?, and who?" about anything that moves or the many things that don't.

Children teach adults to be silly, to be imaginative, and to look beyond the spilled milk or chocolate coated hands and face.

They teach us to have patience as their little feet can travel only so fast and their hands can only reach so high.

Children even teach us to be photographers, to hurry and get that Kodak moment.

Latter on in life our children teach us that sitting next to their brother or sister for that Kodak moment wasn't all that bad. The pictures left behind created life touching moments that we treasure for a life time.

Children teach their fathers that small fish are the big catch of the day for them.

Children also teach us that their infectious giggles can spread throughout a room in a short time.

Anyway you look at it, children teach us many valuable lessons in life.

You Are Right

One day a parochial school teacher brought to school a picture, a book, and a candle in a votive cup.

This being the fourth grade class she thought they may absorb more by showing them an article of what she wanted them to learn, instead of lecturing them.

The class was very quiet as she was arranging her items on the table. The teacher held up the picture and questioned, "who is this person?" A little boy raised his hand and answered, "His name is Jesus."

The Teacher said, 'You're right." The teacher went to the next raised hand.

A little girl said in a quiet voice, "He was born in a manger many years ago, and everybody came to see him because he was a special baby."

The teacher said, "You're right."

Another student almost leapt out of his desk saying, "Jesus picture is hanging on one of the walls in my home, and when we go to church on Sunday I see him in church."

"Where do you see him in church?" The teacher questioned.

The little boy replied with confidence, 'I see him in front of church nailed to a cross. He died for everyone's sins, and he loves all of us even when we're naughty. He loves little kids like me, and moms and dads, even grandpa and grandmas."

"You're right."

A little girl started to giggle and anxiously raised he hand. "At meal time, bedtime, and when I go to church I fold my hands and so does the rest of my family and we pray to him."

The teacher said, "You're right."

The teacher looked at the picture and continued. "This is a picture of Jesus and Jesus did die for all of us on the cross for our sins because he loved us.

If we do wrong he will forgive us. He's with us all and watching over us and guiding us to be good people."

Next the teacher held up a black book and asked, "What is the name of this book and why should we read it?"

A little boy replied, "I have one of those books in my home. My mom and dad read it all the time. It's the Bible. My mom and dad like it."

A little girl, in a spirited voice, said, "We read from it at Christmas time. You know, the story about baby Jesus. My dad says he's the best gift we ever received at Christmas time."

A little boy stood up, looked at the teacher and said, "That book is the best book you can ever read because it's all truth. It tells us how to be good and what to do and what not to do. When we have little troubles and big troubles the Bible has answers for them."

"You're right. The Bible is a true book and it guides us every day to be good people. All we have to do is read it, and it will help us."

The teacher then lit the candle in the votive cup. The teacher asked, "What does this candle mean to you?"

One little boy raised his hand and said, "I think this is what it means. When you are naughty, we seem to be in darkness and when we ask Jesus to forgive us we are in the light.

The Bible is like when the sun is out. When we read it, our face starts to smile. It makes us happy. It's like turning our bedroom light on so we can see where we're going so we don't trip and fall.

The light shows us where to go so we are safe."

A little girl raised her hand and spoke softly, "I think it means that we are to be the light of the world. We are supposed to get others excited about Jesus and his words from the Bible."

A little boy walked up to the candle and put his hands near the flame and said, "Teacher, the candle makes me feel warm, like my blanket at home. My mom says Jesus puts his arms around us when things aren't going so good and he walks with us."

The teacher said, "The candle brings light to our path so we don't stumble and fall. We are to stay on a good path and when we go off the path, that is when trouble is all around us and we don't know what to do or where to turn."

A little boy stood up and screamed, "I've been in a lot of trouble and that's no fun at all!" My mom and dad were sad, and mad, you should've heard them! After all that, I was a good boy. My prayers were really long that night.

The next day I asked my mom and dad if they were still mad at me and they both hugged and held me so tight I could hardly breathe. They both had a big smile on their faces and told me they wanted me on the right path. They told me next to think about what I'm doing and if it doesn't feel right not to do it."

The teacher smiled at the class and then took a second look at one of the students. He had a pencil in his hand and a piece of paper with a drawing on it. The boy had a smile on his face as he stared at what he drew.

The teacher questioned the student. "The piece of paper in your hand, is it something you would like to share with the class?"

The boy gave a cheerful smile and then stood up with his drawing. He brought it to the front of the class to show everyone. He then said, "In my home we have no picture of Jesus, we have no Bible, and we have no candles. This picture that I drew will be hung on the refrigerator. I drew a picture of Jesus, the Bible, and a candle. When my mom and dad ask me what I drew I will tell them. I will also tell what

all of the pictures mean."

The teacher paused and said to the student, "Very good, but I have one more thing I would like to see added to your sheet."

The student agreed and got his pencil out and wrote what the teacher said, "In the darkness of our world, we have many more candles to light."

If, I Would Have Only

Dedicated in Honor
(To: Diane Gustad of Winsted, MN) (Friend)

"If," is such a small word, yet we questioned ourselves everyday using that small little word, "If ".

"If," I would have done that. "If," I would have took the time. "If," I would have been there. "If," I would have helped out. "If," I would have said something. The list goes on and on.

The little word, "If," even becomes a choice in life for us. To stand and do nothing or to walk away from something without acknowledgement, nothing becomes nothing, because nothing happened. There was no action taken. "If," wasn't in action at the specific time.

However, if we put "If," into action we experience and see results from the tiny little word.

"If," we didn't have falling rain, we wouldn't experience the beauty of the rainbow.

"If," we didn't plant a seed, we wouldn't experience the growth of what became the outcome of the tiny seed.

"If," we didn't lend a hand in time of need to others, we wouldn't experience someone offering a hand to us in our time of need.

"If," we didn't have tears, we wouldn't experience someone holding us as our tears landed on their shoulder.

"If," we didn't smile at one another, we wouldn't experience that returned smile.

"If," we didn't love one another, we wouldn't experience happiness because, hate turns into a cold heart and builds a solid wall.

"If," we didn't communicate we, would never experience the warmth of touching another person's soul.

"If," we didn't share our gifts with others, we wouldn't experience God's unique individual design.

"If," we didn't share our thoughts with others we, wouldn't experience the vision of another person's idea of making the world a better place to be in.

"If," we didn't pause for a moment throughout our day we, wouldn't experience God's voice whispering to us and guiding us on our way.

"If," we didn't help the needy we, wouldn't experience what it was like to be poor.

"If," we didn't share God's Word with others we, wouldn't experience what the Bible has to offer to everyone.

"If " we didn't have a friend we, wouldn't experience the comforting and uplifting words of a treasured friend.

"If," we didn't care about others we, wouldn't experience the feelings and emotions of another persons pain.

"If," we didn't forgive one another we, wouldn't experience the rebuilding of trust within two human beings.

"If " we didn't pray we, wouldn't experience God at work in the world around us.

In other words, "If," we don't put our "If," into action, nothing is nothing, were only standing still wondering, "If," I would have only responded and motivated myself, an experience would have nested within the soul and heart.

SHAPING OUR ATTITUDE

It was the middle of September and the Art Teacher wanted to try an experiment on her 9th grade class as, they were starting to challenge her temperament.

The students were starting to complain, some showed signs of boredom, while some had an attitude that was something to be desired.

The Teacher looked at all of her students and said to them, "You are all starting to show signs of having a bad attitude and we have just begun the school year."

The students started to rearrange themselves, this got their attention. The Teacher announced to the students, "Every morning that each one of us gets up, we decide right their, what kind of day were going to have. Our attitude is 100% a part of all of us everyday."

The students started to stir in their seats and laughter came from all directions.

The Teacher laid a handful of clay on each of the students desk.

The Teacher could see excitement in their eyes, this looked like fun.

The Teacher began speaking, "Everyday we all have an important job before we come to school. Our job is to choose what kind of a day were going to have."

"Today we can complain that we had to come to school or we can eagerly open our mind and fill it with tidbits of knowledge."

"Today we all can complain about the rain or we can be thankful the grass is getting watered and will soon turn green."

"Today we can complain about our health or we can rejoice that we are alive."

"Today we can think about all our parents didn't give us while we were growing up or we can be grateful our parents allowed us to be born."

"Today we can complain about the cold lunch or we can be happy we have food before us to eat."

"Today we can complain and feel sad that we don't have any money or we can think wisely about our next purchase."

"Today we can complain about helping around our homes or we can be grateful we have shelter over our head."

"With your clay you are the sculptor. You can flatten your clay and be a dead beat or you can form your clay and shape yourself and be the best with attitude and all. What will today be like is up to you. You get to choose and shape what kind of day you will want to have."

The students had much to think about while shaping their clay to their own thoughts.

The Art Teacher discovered the class had learned much, for she had many pleasant days following this experiment.

Show And Tell

One day a 3rd grade teacher was surrounded by her students, they had a important question for their teacher.

A little boy blurted out, "Teacher when can we have show and tell?"

The teacher was astounded by the question. She then looked at all the 3rd graders as they all had a questionable look on their face as, they bobbed up and down waiting for an answer.

The teacher with a smile on her face replied, "Let's plan to have show and tell tomorrow."

The children all jumped up and down with excitement. They started to chat back and forth in wonder what each one was going to bring.

The next day came and the children were still very excited about having show and tell.

Some had brown paper bags, some had back packs, and some had boxes of all shapes and sizes with their show and tell inside.

Row by row each student got to present their show and tell item.

Some of the children brought toys from home, some brought their sports pictures, some brought their favorite movie or DVD. It was exciting to see what each child had interest in and what was of importance to them.

The teacher was proud of her class, for it was a time of learning, discovery, and adventure.

A little girl did, however, touched the heart of her classmates and the teacher was without words when she showed her show and tell items.

The little girl stood up and in her hand she held a adult purse and began to tell her story. She said, "Do you like it?" The boys chuckled and the girls were oohing and awhing.

The little girl smiled and began speaking, "This is a very special purse. It's made of pure leather and it has a lot of zippers to hold many things."

She unzipped one of the zippers and pulled out a mirror. "My mother told me that little girls should always look at themselves and make sure they look nice. Little girls should be pretty inside and outside. We should make sure we are a good reflection to others. My mother said the mirror should last me a life time."

Next the little girl reached in her purse and held in her hand a recipe card. "This is a recipe that's my mothers favorite and I find it to be my favorite also. When I get older I will be able to make it anytime I want and share it with others."

She then pulled out a package of Kleenex's and told the class, "These are very much needed in a purse. You can blow your nose, wipe your glasses, clean up little spills, and wipe your tears."

The little girl reached in a side pocket and held in her hand some lip stick. She took the cover off and said boldly, "This is lip stick and it's to be used when I am older, not now. Some things that we get in life are to be used when we are older. I have to wait a long time, my mother told me."

The little girl reached in and pulled out a pocket hand sized New Testament Bible. She held it up and looked directly at her teacher and replied, "My mother said that in time I will become a good reader by staying in school. I will learn great things from this little Bible. What I will learn will stay with me for a life time."

Then the little girl did something that the teacher thought was a bit strange. The little girl went to a kneeling position and gently cradled the purse. The little girl started to cry. The teacher wrapped her arms around the little girl and whispered in her ear. "I want you to open the next zipper and tell us what you have in your purse."

The little girl reached for one of the Kleenex's and wiped her eyes. She looked at the class and said, "See, I'm already using my show and tell items, from my purse in class. I have only three more items in my purse."

"I have a pen and paper to write notes so people will know where I am at all times. This is important no matter how old you are." The little girl looked at her note pad and gave a sigh and said, "My note pad already has a note to me from my mother."

Another classmate questioned, "What does the note say?"

Tears came to the little girls eyes. She wiped a tear that was about to make a landing and replied, "The note says, whenever you find something that is small and of value to either help yourself in need or others, put it in this special purse.

Everyday you will be helping yourself or some one else in life's journey."

Finally, the little girl said, "In my hand I hold the last thing I have in my purse." It was a key. The little girl held up the single key and showed it to her classmates.

A little boy asked, "What's the key for?"

The girl responded, "I have one key and my mother has the other interlocking key to this one.

My mother promised me that one day these two keys will interlock together again.

My mother went to heaven. She's really far away. I have the key to her heart and she has the key to mine."

The little girl slowly shuffled her feet back to her seat.

The teacher told the class, "You must all realize you weren't just looking at a leather purse. You were looking at a purse that a Mother new that she was going away and would not be around to help her daughter. Her mother put what was important in this purse to help bring delight to someone, including her daughter. The teacher realized that this show and tell wasn't just about learning, discovery, and adventure. It was about a little girl who was wrapped up in her Mother's love."

Fall The Beauty Of God's Handy Work (October)

God's Colorful World

Dedicated in Honor To:
Sue Dressel of Waconia, MN
(Former Front Desk Secretary at the Herald
Journal in Winsted MN – Friend)

This time of the year we are blessed with God's colorful handiwork.

The red, orange, yellow, green, brown, and purple leaves on the trees are complimentary to one another.

Day after day the leaves change colors. Their rich colors finish out the growing season in a brilliant display of spectacular fall colors.

Within time every crisp leaf makes it's way to the ground. In time the trees are bare. For a short time we observe and admire God's work of art.

Imagine what our world would be like without color. How dull our surroundings would be.

The fall season sends a message. It stimulates and excites us. It visibly shows us that were in the midst of seasonal change.

The squirrels are gathering food. Our gardens are at rest. Flowers wither and hide themselves. The grapes have been picked and all that remains is the vine. The apples have been picked and all that remains are the branches. The crops have been harvest and all that remains are the dark rustic fields.

Our weather becomes cooler. Everyday we live in the process of nature telling us were in the process of changing to the next season.

Year after year we adapt and learn to except the environment of seasonal change.

One of the greatest messages ever told is that God does not change. He never hides or with draws himself from us. He does not rest. He remains strong for us in our needs year round. He is our strength and is powerful without change. (Malachi 3:6.) God displays His beauty just like the fall leaves and is complimentary to us.

God is with us 24 hours a day, 7 days out of a week, and 365 days out of a year displaying His beauty to each and every one of us.

BEING PRACTICAL

There once was a man that came from another country to live in the states. He was of a calm and serene character.

Most people frequently found him among the poor, diseased, and the lonely.

He was offering something most people had a hard time doing. He would walk up to the people and offer them a touch of hope, and gently touched them. He extended to them a simple word of encouragement, and said a few words to up-lift them. He looked them in their eyes and gave them a warm smile. This was precious as none of these acts of kindness cost him a cent. It did however, raise the value of him as a person of good character in God's eyes.

The next day, he was found in government buildings talking to high powerful people negotiating with educated people. They valued his words and plan of action he wanted for mankind that was less fortunate then himself. He spoke in their behalf and the powerful understood the intent of him coming their, to help those wants and needs.

At night time he would put puzzles together or make simple wooden crafts to give away.

He was a basic and practical person, prestige never entered his mind. He was never distracted from his humbleness. His mind was set on structuring his life around God's priorities and purposes. He wanted to be considered a person in the world, but not of the world.

MAKE EVERY DAY SPECIAL

When I was small we traveled often.

We passed the time while driving by admiring the beautiful fall trees.

We also found it amusing to read the signs along the road. The signs were there to help us chart the way; "Food, lodging, next right", "Lake Serra 10 miles."

Sometimes warnings: "Watch for falling rocks", "Curves next two miles."

Sometimes detours take us places we don't want to go.

Our lives are often referred to as a journey. A journey of expectations, milestones, excursions, detours, joys and sorrows.

From the beginning we are continually looking ahead. We can't wait for those first steps, the first tooth, the first day of school, the sixteenth birthday, graduation, career, marriage, children, grandchildren, retirement, and on and on it goes.

Sometimes we think more about the trip than the destination. One day I saw a little girl, about four years old, at the convenience store counter with her mother. While her mother was buying supplies for the trip, the little girl could hardly hold still. She was literally dancing she was so excited.

"Where are you going?" the clerk asked the little girl.

"To Grandma's!" she shouted. She didn't say North Dakota. The place didn't matter. As far as she was concerned she was going to a person.

119

She was bearing witness to the fact that we home in those we love and who love us. In people more than places.

During Christ's life on earth, again and again he told us, John 14:2-3, "In my Father's house are many mansions: If it were not so, I would have told you. I go to prepare a place for you. And if I prepare a place for you, I will come again, and receive you unto myself: that where I am, there ye may be also."

We should celebrate those milestones and markers on our journey. Make every day special. Celebrate also those whose lives have gone before us as they begin a never ending life in Jesus Christ.

May we always remember who we belong to and to whom we are going.

Living Each Day At A Time

As we greet each morning, most of us are consistently following a pattern or daily routine of what we need to do in order to get ourselves motivated for the start-up of our day.

Most of us have heard the little statement, "Take one day at a time, don't worry about tomorrow for tomorrow isn't here."

If we choose to live one day at a time in thought, in our actions, in our motives, we may then question the day were living in.

Did we do something today that was worth living?

Did we do some sort of unselfish giving or deed to another person? Did we bring joy or happiness to another person? Did we convey our words with compassion or honesty? Did we inflict a wound or heal a wound? Did we lighten another person's load, physically, or mentally? Did we strengthen or cheer another person within our day?

Did we radiate light and love as we moved through our day? Did we walk peacefully and with acceptance?

As evening falls and were at the close of our day, what did we do to make that day worth living?

There are no two days that are the same. We all get one chance to learn and discover about our individual day.

This is no magic or illustrated book that will ever be able to show or tell anyone of us how our day is going to be.

We may even question each other with, "How's your day going? or How are you today?"

There's a great possibility someone was intending to find a way to make your day much brighter, that is why they asked you.

Everyday we should be living in unity with each other.

The healthy side of living is knowing were all linked together as humans. Our short comings only prove were human and learning from our actions within our day.

None of us are perfect or will ever have a perfect day. Our days are designed for us to learn, discover, correct, and to uplift those around us, even those we do not know.

Many obstacles may come our way within our day. However, help is on the way, for there are those who are equipped to wrestle with what we don't understand and make our day more calmer.

When we all use our God given gifts to help others were on a road to helping mankind survive.

Everyone of us makes hundred of choices every day. Every choice we make has an impact on our lives and the lives of others.

Everyday we need to see the beauty in the world.

Accept yourself for what you are and at the same time we should balance the need between self acceptance and growth.

In our individual day, "Who comforteth us in all our tribulation, that we may be able to comfort them which are in any trouble, by the comfort wherewith we ourselves are comforted of God." 2 Corinthians 1:4

A Quilt A Gift Of Love

The fall season is a time when we find ourselves most comfortable when snuggled in a home-made quilt.

The amazing part of the quilt is that, there just old or new scrapes of perfectly good fabric, sewn together to make a blanket that provides us with warmth and comfort.

To sit around a quilting frame with a needle in your hand is an awakening experience, one needs to acknowledge the time and effort involved in the art of quilting. Quilting is of patience a gift from God enter twined with a touch of his great Blessings forward on to another person.

Quilts are pieces of fabric sewn together like moments in time. The working together makes people feel like part of a community, giving them the chance to connect, self expression, tell stories, sing songs, and enjoy each others company as they sewed. Quilting is a unique project that reflects our true self. Sometimes the fabric brings a memory to our quilt, as hand-made as life itself.

Every quilt has a story to tell and are made with decorative designs that brings a tear to our eyes and warmth to our heart that lasts forever.

Some quilts delivers a message of friendship and love in every word spoken.

Some quilts offer encouragement and compassion for the places in our lives that need to be wrapped in comfort.

Every stitch is done in love and hand crafted in beauty for all to admire.

123

The rich earth tone colors neutralize our thoughts, while the bold color designs bring excitement, drama, illusion, visual, and adventure to our thoughts.

Quilts are hand crafted in many designs, an art that lives on, in the hearts of many who receive one as a gift.

Many quilts find a way of discovering our personal and family roots as well as a collective past.

Countless people donate many hours to make something to comfort someone they'll never meet who may be going through a difficult time. Many quilts are made to raise funds for an important cause.

Many quilters spend their time, a part of their lives, on the making of a quilt, so that in its giving, they give part of themselves, and in the receiving of a quilt, a person accepts a gift like no other.

Our lives are quilted together by the artwork of God's design.

Those that sleep under a hand-made quilt sleep under a blanket of love.

To those of you who have ever been a part of a hand-made quilt, there are meaningful words for you, "wherever a beautiful soul has been, there is a trail of beautiful memories."

We quilt to celebrate and commemorate, cherish, dream, hope, remember, connect, care, and love.

A Time For Giving Thanks (November)

Be Thankful Everyday

With the holiday season now upon us, it's easy to get all caught up in the hustle and bustle of the holiday and forget to give thanks for all of the greatest gifts each of us have been blessed with.

On Thanks-giving Day there are many of us who sit shoulder to shoulder at the dinner table with friends and loved ones, casual acquaintances, even strangers.

Before we reach for the bread and butter, mashed potatoes, or gravy ladle, many of us will pause for a few words of thanks for all we're surrounded with.

If we didn't celebrate Thanksgiving Day most of us would continue in our busy mode and wouldn't realize the impact of all that we have been blessed with.

We find it so easy to take things for granted, or sometimes we don't appreciate the little things other do for us.

Every day, with little reminders to ourselves, may our attitude reflect a surge of confidence that it is our responsibility to take our God-given talents and make a difference daily.

On Thanksgiving Day we should all be reminded that we should not only be thankful for what we have been blessed with within that day.

We should also be grateful and thankful for the promise of more blessings to come.

SERVING AND BEING SERVED

Thanksgiving time is a time when the words, to be thankful and giving thanks come to our minds. Although, it seems to mean something different to almost everyone.

What to be thankful for can be a wide spread of things from our jobs, health, home, food, money, clothing, friends, and family. However, may we all be thankful for all we are blessed with.

In order to really enjoy and recognize our greatest blessings that we are surrounded with, we must all learn to take time to stop, slow down, pause, prioritize, and let our soul reflect upon what's connected to our inner most being.

In today's world porch swings, picnic tables, and handwritten letters are slowly becoming a part of the bygone age.

We are now faced with fast-food drive through, computer games, and email. We are never than a beeper or cellular phone call away from being summoned.

A lot of people are working endless hours a week. This is a sign of first class exhaustion.

We need to balance our lives and find enjoyment in each other and search for the underlining of happiness and sorrow within our loved ones.

The purpose of life is not just to get things done but, more so, to connect with each other.

Many of us hear or say the words, "Thank You," throughout the day, somewhere or someplace. Just two words meaning, I appreciate what you did for me, or what you said in goodness on behalf of another person. The sincerity that was spoken uplifted another person's spirit, whether it be to aid or reach out and be of cheer or comfort.

Passion is important and so is compassion. Helping others was something Jesus did on a daily basis. He was constantly approached by people, but he always found time to stop what he was doing to help those in need. This is a lesson we must learn if we want to be anything like Jesus.

Hands are referred to numerous times in the bible. God's hands created the heavens and the earth. Jesus laid his hands on many; lepers were healed and the blind made to see by his touch. His hands were nailed in his sacrifice on the cross for our sins and were lifted to bless his disciples before his accent to heaven. Our hands are to carry on his work.

We don't perform miracles, but we can lend a hand to benefit others. We may offer a steady hand to the elderly, a strong hand to make repairs, a creative hand to make clothing or quilts for the homeless, a warm outstretched hand to a stranger, a clasping hand to a friend, or

folded hands to praise him or give thanks to him.

God sends people to help us when we need them. Sometimes you are the person giving the help and sometimes you are the one receiving it; both roles are important. The operative word is person. It's about people, not things. Knowing, more than doing. Being, more than getting.

Every day may we all be of some sort of service somehow, or somewhere.

Search and you will find something to be thankful for and also be blessed with. To find silence and to reflect upon our day, we will realize that all along Jesus was our example: The greatest work ever begun upon this earth was planned and started by Jesus.

Being Thankful For More

Blessings To Come

Dedicated in Honor
(To: Sarah Franke of Waconia, Mn.) (Friend)

We live from day to day in a fast paced world, it's non stop every where we go.

Some don't even take the time to think about the blessings that have been bestowed upon them. There utilizing all their energy running here and running there.

Some of us don't even realize a blessing if we saw one right in front of us.

A blessing is clearly something that has been given to you from God himself. He finds it in his best interest to share it with you.

Some may question have I been blessed or have I been over- looked by God?

We are never over-looked by God, he's just in the process of doing what He wants in his time not our time.

We are all blessed with at least one of these, children, family, friends, homes, food, clothing, jobs, health, schools, churches, and many more should be added to the list.

If, there was a crystal ball in front of us, to tell us what are next blessing was going to be, that would be wonderful, but there is none and never will be.

We just need to pause a little through-out our day and seek them out.

It's amazing what we would all see we have been blessed with.

On our journey in life many unexpected blessings will come to us. We will be joyous, excited and filled to the brim in happiness. God has his ways of diligently pouring his great blessings into the laps of mankind.

We all need to realize we live in a world where there will be more blessings to come to brighten our day and bring us to realize there is a God that's sharing his ultimate plan with each and everyone of us. He wants us to know He does bless his creation.

The Art Of Thinking

We all know there aren't any two people who think the same. The thought might be if, we relaxed and altered our thoughts a little, would our days be somewhat more enjoyable?

When adults see the fall trees, we think of the cold weather, icy roads, and snow that on it's way.

A child will see beautiful colored leaves. They collect and use the leaves for school projects and to run and jump in, this is a fun time for them.

When adult see a homeless person, they see a smelly, dirty person who wants money and proceed to walk the other way.

A child will see a homeless person and will smile at them and will get a returned smile.

When adults see running children, they say, "don't run, you might get hurt."

A child feels joyous to use their legs to run, jump, and skip. They are on a adventure exploring their surroundings.

When an adult sees a child with chocolate hands and face, they see a mess to clean-up including their clothes.

A child is excited he/she got to feed himself/herself and was the center of attention, while everybody laughed. This was fun play time for them.

When adults feel wind on their face, we brace ourselves against it. We feel it's messing up our hair and pulling us back as we walk.

A child will close their eyes, spread their arms and fly with it, until they fall to the ground laughing.

When adults see their child go off to school for the first time, they feel lost, sad, and like the world has crumbled at their feet.

A child is excited with the new clothes, the new school bag and wanting to meet their new friends.

When a adult sees a child introduced to something new, we think they might not be able to do it without our help.

A child smiles and is excited and curious about something new they get to try to achieve or learn by exploring.

When adults pray, we have many things we want and give me this and give me that.

A child will say, "Hi God, thanks for all my new toys and my friends. Bless my family and my puppy."

When adults see a mud puddle, we step around it. We see muddy shoes and clothes and tracked up floors.

A child will sit in it. They will run threw it. They will see play time with building dams and rivers to cross and worms to play with.

At some point, an adult might wonder, if we are given children to teach or to learn from.

The Biggest Change Starts

With Ourselves

I n our everyday living we are at some point in our lives geared towards the thought of, "what can I do to improve, to make better, to change, about my life or life style?"

The word, "change," is a very delicate word and sometimes next to impossible to do for some.

We must at times, accept that we are living in a changing world, nothing stays the same, other than God. God will not change and God does not change.

We all want to be attached to something that makes us feel comfortable and stable. Jesus is that little piece that we are looking for that needs to be interlocked to each and everyone of us individually. To understand all people and their feelings to change is hard to obtain and next to impossible.

Some people love change, live for change, and some choose not to change, that's when you see the walls come tumbling down.

We all have wants, needs, and desires. The greatest factor is, how does what I want, need or desire effect me as a person and the world as a whole?

It's been said, "the biggest change starts with ourselves."

Everyday we are faced with many decisions and challenges. We are all responsible and accountable for what we say and do.

Every time we speak our character is on a pedestal being displayed. Our character and integrity defines what are true side is all about. Jesus was our perfect example. When Jesus spoke, He spoke the truth, He lived a compassionate life, He spoke to correct, He spoke and shared the gospel with others.

When Jesus used His hands, He built many things being a carpenter.

He touched the blind using the mud and the spittle, so they could see again.

His hands served others. His mission on earth was not to serve himself.

His hands calmed the winds and the sea. He fed the 5,000, He turned water into wine, a miracle at hand.

His hands carried the cross that He himself was nailed too. A nail in each hand did a job no other human could do for the entire world.

Jesus didn't change his mind and abandoned us. He loved us and changed the world by His dying on the cross.

His hands held the little children as He blessed them one by one.

To a quiet place He went only to find Him with his hands folded in prayer.

All our many prayers technically find us in a changing world. God is in control of all change. He has the method of rearranging all of us to where he wants us to be and do His will while we are here on earth.

Jesus is the Reason for the Season (December)

Jesus Is The Reason

For The Season

As we prepare for the Christmas holiday, it's apparent that it's a very busy time of the year and sometimes, it can be a little overwhelming.

There's the cooking, cleaning, indoor and outdoor decorating, church and school Christmas programs, Christmas cards, the traditional business parties, and gift buying for loved ones.

The store ads shout the holiday sale prices at us. We check one thing off our to-do list and add three more. Even thinking about all our activities can exhaust us, but we still walk forward in excitement for the Christmas holiday season.

Most of us do something in family tradition for the holidays. The Advent calendar is a tradition in many Christian families. The calendar can be a picture of a Christian scene, covered with numbered flaps. Each day, the children open a flap to reveal hidden Advent scenes.

A Christmas store once offered an Advent calendar with a lovely nativity scene on the front. Behind each flap, however, were pieces of chocolate and the picture of a toy. On Dec. 24, the manger opened the flap to reveal a chocolate Santa-hardly what the shepherds found in Bethlehem. Our analogy in thoughts should be, soldiers fight, teachers teach, accountants add, pastors preach. Fathers, mothers, sisters, brothers-no matter who we are, we have duties to perform. At Bethlehem God sent Jesus to redeem the world from sin. On the last day, God will send Jesus to abolish all evil and complete his perfect kingdom, for eternity in heaven. These are Jesus' duties, and he performs them flawlessly.

In all that we do this holiday season, may we reflect our thoughts on the baby Jesus, who lay in swaddling clothes in the manger, for there was no room for him in the inn. Many came from afar, following the brightest star of all, to see the greatest star of all, to see the greatest gift of all, Baby Jesus.

May we all have a blessed Christmas and ponder these thoughts, "Jesus is the reason for the season."

Decorating For The

Christmas Season

This time of the year most of us are excited about the Christmas season.

We search for our Christmas decorations in the attic or basement. All the boxes and totes are filled with Christmas lights, ornaments, tree stand, tree top, tree skirt, nativity set, candy dishes, our favorite figurine, including all the special momentous we received from family and friends over the years. These are especially nice because they have been stored with memories over the years.

Perhaps you unwrap a homemade ornament that your daughter Susie, made. The response would most likely be, "Oh Susie, look what I found. You made this for me in second grade." You hold it in your hands, gently pondering over the ornament with glistening eyes, and your heart pounds with excitement. It is something the hands of your child has made for you.

It becomes one-of-a-kind, with no price tag or dollar amount big enough for another person to purchase.

The garland and wreath are hung. The pine scent spreads within your home. The nativity is arranged, with each figurine having their special place within the stable.

The most important piece, however, is the baby Jesus. He is the center of attraction for all to see and bless. With all the beauty of the Christmas season, we need to be decorating our hearts, as well.

We may send a card, give someone a gift, or telephone a friend or family at a distance.

We may send a few kind words, or we find some quiet time with God, thanking him for all that He has done for us.

Our reflection may be as beautiful inside as the world appears outside of us.

Our Names Have Meaning

As children the first word we write is our name.

A child, in the beginning may write the "E" this way and that way. The "N" maybe written backwards. The "T" may be crossed where he/ she feels it's right for the moment.

The child is very happy when told, "you spelled your name correctly." As we become adults our name appears on checks, letters, mortgages, contracts, debit cards, licenses, etc.

Most often we are offended when someone spells, or says, our name incorrectly.

We defend the name we have been given, because it's the name we've been given for life.

It has always been a privilege to name our children at birth.

We write the many different names, and say the names many times, until we find the name we will cherish for our child.

Every name has a meaning for that particular name.

When Mary was expecting, Joseph was told by God to take Mary home as his wife.

Joseph was very excited about the thought of parenting this child.

He would teach him to read and write.

He would work beside him in the carpenter shop, get water from the well, play with him in the hills of Galilee, tuck him in at night and say his prayers with him.

It was only natural that Joseph wanted to name the child. He wanted the same privilege. Maybe Joseph would want to name him Joseph Jr., David, Paul, or Jacob after his grandfather.

He to had many names picked out without knowing God had different ideas.

God, through an angel, announced to Joseph, "Mary will give birth to a son, and you will give him the name Jesus because he will save his people from their sins." Matthew 1:21

Joseph was astounded by the news. He couldn't comprehend those wishes for his son.

A son was born unto Mary. She wrapped him in swaddling clothes and laid him in a manger.

He was respectfully named Jesus. Mary and Joseph knew there was something special about the baby.

A star shown brightly so others could find baby Jesus.

People gathered around, coming from afar to see that which was born.

The wise men brought their gifts, the shepherds gathered around to see the prince of peace.

Jesus grew up. When he taught, his students were amazed. When he touched the sick, they were healed.

Those who tried to accuse him, couldn't find a flaw in him.

His disciples didn't always understand his ways but they found no other alternative but to believe in him.

His miracles were without dispute, his character was of integrity, his words were unforgettable, his love was poured out to all, his compassion extended to the heart and soul of his people, his suffering was a loss for words, his resurrection was undeniable. For someone to reject him was unthinkable. Jesus fulfilled every promise God foreshadowed to us. Jesus dotted every "I" and crossed every "T" saying, "It is finished."

He completed his father's plan. May we never forget the baby's name and all that it stood for.

He is Immanuel, God with us, wonderful counselor, mighty God, everlasting father, prince of peace.

He suffered. His hands were pierced for our transgressions and crushed for our iniquities. He's untouchable, but his love, messages, and the fragrance of him spread beyond each and every one of us daily.

The Evergreen Christmas
Tree Lives On

A little girl was standing in the darkness of their living room admiring their fully decorated Christmas Tree.

Her eyes glistened as she watched the tree lights blink on and off. The ornaments were of one of a kind. Some ornaments had glitter on them, some were made of ceramic, some were made of wood and some were singing ornaments.

The little girl smiled when she saw the special ones. The special ones were hand-maid and had their own uniqueness. She happened to spot a few she had made with her own little hands. She chuckled when she saw all the extra dried on glue she used, to hold her ornament together.

The tinsel sparkled from the top of the tree to the bottom of the tree.

At the top of the tree was a animated angel. She was lit up and would move her arms back and forth.

The mother came into the room and was observing her daughter and became curious, she asked her daughter,

"you look amused by something." The little girl nodded her head and replied back to her mother,

"I was just thinking. Why isn't the Christmas Tree a apple tree, or a maple tree? Why does it always have to be a Evergreen Tree?" The mother smiled and replied. "The Christmas Tree will always be a Evergreen Tree. The other trees loose their leaves or their fruit, come the fall season.

The Evergreen Tree is always green for as long as they grow and has the pleasant aroma of the forest. It's something like Christ's love for us, it never changes and is always there."

The little girl smiled at her mothers answer.

The mother then continued, "The Christmas tree years ago started out with popcorn strung on a string. It was considered the garland for the tree and then latter on the tree was removed from the indoors and put outside so the birds could eat the popcorn from the tree. Today, the garland comes in many styles, shapes, sizes and colors.

They used to have edible fruit, cranberries and ginger bread cookies hung on the tree in place of the ornaments we have today. The tree top has been everything from baby Jesus, to the star, to an angel.

Instead of light bulbs, they used to put lit candles on the tree in honor of Christ's Birth, until to many homes had fires. We now continue with the light bulbs in many different colors. Some enjoy the blinking lights and some don't. The Evergreen tree always bears lights at Christmastime in memory of the night it gave such pleasure to the Baby Jesus.

Some put a light coat of artificial snow on the tree to give it a touch of winter wonder land.

It's amazing how many things have changed but the Evergreen tree will always remain as God's love for us never changes, it too still remains the same. Hebrews 13:8 "Jesus Christ the same yesterday, and today, and forever."

Gifts To Share

E veryone has special gifts to give. Within time, we learn that the sharing of those gifts can give a person one of the best kinds of feelings you can feel.

The above words bring my thoughts to a little boy. He was the son of a shepherd. His family didn't have much money; therefore, they were not able to buy toys.

The boy spent his time helping his father tend to the sheep in the pastures, and there was not much time for playing.

One day, the boy went with his father to the market in town. As they were passing by stands where people sold their goods, the little boy spotted a beautiful drum, with silver rings around it and a gleaming white top.

He stared at it a long time because he wanted it very badly, but he didn't say anything because he knew that his family could not buy toys for him. His father paused, watching his son staring at the drum, and he knew what he was thinking.

That night, after the son had come in from the pastures where he was helping with the sheep, he ate his supper and went up to get ready for bed.

There, on his bed, sat the beautiful drum he wanted so badly.

The next day, and every day thereafter, the little boy carried the drum with him and practiced on it as he went out to the pastures with the sheep. Both the sheep and the shepherds became accustomed to the drumming, and in time, the boy became quite good at it.

One day, a very poor family came to the area, looking for a place to stay. The young women was pregnant and ready to have her baby any day.

They needed shelter, but were unable to find any in the village below. The boy's family allowed the poor family to stay in their stable.

The poor family was very nice to the young boy, and they were so poor that the boy felt he wanted to give them something special in return for their kindness. But he had nothing to give them.

One cold night, the boy awoke to a bluish light shining in his window. He got up and looked outside, where he saw the stars shining more brightly than he had ever seen before.

The pastures below were even lit up with the starlight so that you could see the sheep clearly, even from afar. It gave the boy a magical feeling.

The shepherds, watching the sheep, were also gathered together, looking up at the unusually bright star. As they were all looking in silence, they heard crying coming from the stable.

The little boy went to look inside, where he saw the mother and the father holding a newborn baby.

The boy suddenly knew what he wanted to give them. He ran upstairs, got his drum, brought it down to the stable, and stepped inside.

He said, "This drum is all I have that is mine, but I want to give it to your baby so when he grows up, he can learn to play like I have." The woman smiled at him, and said, "I've heard you play your drum, and I enjoy it so much that I want you to keep your drum and

share the gift you have for playing, instead."

The boy was very happy to hear that. He picked up his drum and his little lamb nudged him. He began playing, "rum-pum- pum-pum." The Holy child looked at him, and the music the little boy played made the Baby smile. The boy realized his gift was his best- simple, yet

right from his heart.

The best gift we can give is to give of ourselves, a gift we always have to share.

May we pause a moment, to reflect upon the story. Jesus was born unto us; this is a gift to all of us.

Jesus, growing up in life, shared his gifts of carpenter work, teaching, obedience, structure, correction, forgiveness, truth, and God's Holy Word.

Jesus told stories, to bring memories to those around him. He healed many people-the blind, the sick, diseased, fearful, emotional, etc. Jesus' hands were hands to serve, not to be served.

Jesus then gave the most precious gift of all.. himself. He died on the cross for all our sins.

Jesus has no body now on earth…but yours.

Yours are the only hands with which he can do his work. Yours are the only feet with which he can go about the world. Yours are the only eyes through which His compassion can shine forth upon a troubled world. Jesus has no body body-but yours, to share your gifts to others.

About The Author

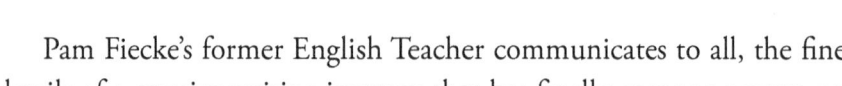

Pam Fiecke's former English Teacher communicates to all, the fine details of a creative writing journey, that has finally come to a wrap-up for all to enjoy!

Although recently retired, I taught English in Lester Prairie High School for 35 years. Even in her junior high years, Pam's creative writing talent was very evident. She quickly learned the fundamentals, and then advanced her style and word choice to make her writing interesting and meaningful. Her love for writing grew as her talent "blossomed". When I would give her one and two page assignments, she would enthusiastically turn in five or more pages. She was an excellent learner, always willing to put- forth the extra effort to create memorable writing. Her description was clear and effective, and her characters were interesting. Her word choice was fresh and vital, always drawing the reader toward a meaningful conclusion. Pam did excellent work.

Pam's creative writing work, under my supervision, culminated with the publication of her first novel within the onset of High School Graduation. (Yesterday's tears becomes tomorrows smiles.) I was-and remain-extremely proud of her.

I welcome Pam's new second book to the "Must Read!" list. Her thirty-year journey from my Creative Writing classroom to this new book offering has been interrupted, but never abandoned. Her Inspirational Stories are positive, hopeful, and uplifting-highly desirable and valuable reading in today's troubled world. Pam has a strong work-ethic, and a optimistic personality. Her love for writing, and her unwavering faith in the irrepressible human spirit have lured her into sharing these stories with us. Her words- without being cutsey or peachy-evoke warm smiles, and gently remind us that being positive and hopeful are necessary keys to achieving happy lives.

Robert D. Henning
Instructor of English, Retired
Lester Prairie Public School, MN

About The Author

Msgr. Robert J. Wyffel's, a former Priest, writes about Pam's efforts within the Religious Education Program while under the direction of himself and the Holy Trinity Parish in Winsted, MN Pam Fiecke was the Sunday School Coordinator during the 15 years that I served as pastor and superintendent at Holy Trinity Parish in Winsted, MN.

I was very pleased with our excellent Sunday School Program under her leadership. Eligible students and families were happy to participate. Pam was certainly very well organized, communicated well with me and the Education Committee and with the parents. Both teachers and students had a good rapport with her. It was easy to follow the schedule she set up.

Pam was very dependable and would have everything organized and ready for every class. She was very generous with her time and able to solicit her family and friends and relatives, and the parents as volunteers. The kids were excited about the activities and found the materials interesting and worthwhile. Parents were involved. They appreciated the programs and performances that the students gave at the end of Mass every couple of months. Her Christmas Programs and Potlucks were enjoyed by everyone. Pam is a very honest person and blessed with personal people talents and abilities.

Pam is a person of good character. She helped set the budget and stayed within the budget each year. Donations were received regularly and put to good use.

Pam helped set the goals of our Sunday School Program to enable us to live and proclaim our Mission. A spirit of joy pervaded the learning atmosphere. She complied with the Handbook and all guidelines and directions of the pastor and Education Committee and Diocesan Education Office. It was a joy to work with her and I am happy to write this for her.

Msgr. Robert J. Wyffels, Pastor
St. Michael's Church
Morgan, MN

About The Author

The Herald-Journal of Winsted, MN. Expresses their thoughts of Pam Fiecke's column and writing career.

"Pam Fiecke is a thoughtful writer who has attracted a loyal audience. She is persistent, reliable and inspiring."

- Lynda Jensen, Dale Kovar, Chris Schultz
Herald-Journal of Winsted, MN.

"Pam has been a friend for most of my life. she has always been a "go-getter" she sets her mind on a task and will see it through completion. Pam is devoted to her family, work, church, and community. These inspirational short stories reflect who she is in her everyday life. Pam relates to people of all ages and is a true inspiration to me, I wish her well in all her endeavors."

-Sarah Franke
Friend
Waconia, MN

"My longtime friend Pam writes from her heart. Her Christian writings are uplifting and thoughtful for many of life's situations."

-Diane Gustad
Friend
Winsted, MN

"I have known Pam for a long time. Her writing is enjoyable and Inspirational. I miss her columns in the local paper."

-Troy Feltmann
Herald Journal of Winsted, MN
Sign Dept. Manager
Cousin - Friend
Lester Prairie, MN

"I first got to know Pam as an active and involved member of some of the community organizations. We ended up working at some of the same events and still due to this day. Pam brings a passion and energy to everything she does. If you are involved in the same event in some way, you will know Pam. Likewise, Pam's writing is active and engaged. She is able to present with a passion that is clear to anyone that reads her work."

- Jason Blashack
(Herald Journal of Winsted, MN, Sales Rep, Friend)
Lester Prairie, MN.

"Pam Fiecke is a dedicated and community-minded author whose passion for what she believes in shines through her writing. With a genuine commitment to sharing inspiration, Pam conveys her unique perspective on life with heartfelt words that leave a lasting impact. Her stories, often centered around her experiences growing up and spending time with family, exude warmth and authenticity.

One can almost envision Pam's big, broad smile as they immerse themselves in her narratives. Hailing from the Midwest, Pam manages to transcend geographical boundaries with her universal themes and relatable anecdotes. Her ability to connect with readers on a personal level makes her writing not just regional but globally appealing.

In essence, Pam Fiecke is more than an author; she is a storyteller who weaves a tapestry of memories, emotions, and life lessons. Her dedication to community, coupled with her genuine love for sharing, makes her a captivating and inspirational presence in the literary world."

- Andrew Meuleners
(Herald Journal on Winsted, MN, Managing Editor, Friend)
Winsted, MN.

"Pam's writings are inspirational, down-to-earth, and easy to understand. She uses everyday experiences for a high message and her stories are full of examples, illustrations, and common sense. They are reinforced with even more truth in real-life experiences."

- Sue Dressel
Friend
Waconia, MN.

My Autobiography

J ust as I was, a child heading off to school like any other insecure child, scared, who am I going to know, my stomach was turning, the school bus was big orange and spacious, and I wanted my mom and my puppy!

I attended a parochial school system at elementary level, that is where I cumulated my strong religious Evangelization background. In school, on a day to day basis, I was loved, encouraged, taught about Jesus, and was built-up like every other student, to have faith and live that faith anchored and armored by the word of God. We, were taught morals, values, integrity, evangelization, and religion in a very concrete way. We lived out our teachings and became a great example to others.

When I was in the 4th grade, our parochial school closed, leaving us with no other option but the public school system. I loved writing, it traveled with me. A piece of paper laid before me and a pencil in my hand. I learned the fundamentals, creative writing 1, creative writing 2, then, excelled to advanced creative writing. Before Graduating from high school, I mastered being an Author of my first Published book by the age of 18. "Yesterday's Tears Become Tomorrows Smiles." My teacher commended me for the excellence in the writing field. Following high school, I continued writing, never abandoning myself from writing, however, I kept myself silent to the public. I took aptitude tests for writing children's books, with returned excellent results. I, was in a Writer Guild Training Session, my discovery was, my skills were equal to that of the Professional Authors.

I, ventured into learning and having a successful background in Business, sales, and service with Home Interiors and Gifts. I was taught many positive tools for success and at the same time I was inspired by the direction and steps I had learned while being in Business.

This led me to having learned different strengths and living a healthy and productive life style as a woman.

In 2004, I was selected as Home Town Hero for my community of Winsted for outstanding service. I have successfully ran, organized, and volunteered with many functions over the years.

In 2005, the Herald Journal Newspaper, Chris Schultz, CEO/Publisher and Dale Kovar, General mgr. phoned me, met with me and handed me a column to continue my Inspirational Stories. Now, I was going to be a columnist! My column was named "Inspirational Thoughts," this is where my writing blossomed and my light was shown more evident.

On my journey, I decided to expand my religious beliefs and became interested in Coordinating and teaching Sunday School at Holy Trinity Church in Winsted. This I did for 21 years. This was a wonderful experience for me and our four children.

In 2006, I decided not to only be a columnist, I wanted to write Momentous Writings for the deceased. I would write a special Inspirational writing and personalize it with their name and the deceased date framed to set up at a wake or a funeral. I have a lit candle and flowers or greenery tucked in front of the framed Inspirational writing. This is a gift to the family in behalf of their loved one.

In 2008, a lot of my writings were Copy Written through Direct Legal and are in the Library of Congress in Washington, D.C.

My son, Brandon and I, participated in Missionary work in a group setting in Jamacia. It was a true experience to see what needs to be done to help others less fortunate than ourselves.

I, worked in manufacturing at Sterner Lighting in Winsted, MN. for 19 1/2 years putting light fixtures together and other needed positions, along with being on their safety committee. They closed their doors permanently. I then headed to Crown College in Hutchinson, MN. to The State of Minnesota Nursing Assistant Registry and became Registered in 2009. I continued as a full-time position of being a "Care Specialist" RA in a Dementia Care setting in Dassel/Darwin, MN. I taught devotions to the elderly, activities and assistant to Ministers that came to visit and administer communion to the elderly. In time I was selected employee of the month. In time they dosed their doors, however, I stayed in the position of Nursing Assistant/ Home Health Aide/PCA. I'm currently working for Dominion Cares out of Hutchinson, MN for many years doing in home care for many communities.

In 2011, I wrote and framed, for Fr. Anthony Hesse,

"Forever you will be my parents." That Fr. Tony signed and gave to Richard and Mary Ann Hesse, his parents. They loved it!

In 2012, our town of Winsted was celebrating their 125th Anniversary. I wrote a beautiful piece and presented it to Steve Stotko, the Mayor of Winsted, he received the writing in honor of the city's 125th Anniversary at a city council meeting. The writing was called, "Winsted' s 125th Anniversary." The writing was set on a shelf and the public was included in reading it whenever they came into the city building.

In great surprise 2012, HILLTOP Records, found my Inspirational writings in the Library of Congress in Washington D.C. Over 12 million people have their work in this building! To me, was like finding a needle in a haystack! They wrote me a letter and wanted me to submit them a few songs to HILLTOP Records to review. I, had never written a song in my life! I, hustled with them and came up with five songs, not even knowing if they were actually Lyrics songs. Shortly I received a reply and they contracted all five of them. I, started with only one, "A Halo and A set of Golden Wings." They put music to my writing. Now, I was officially called a Lyricist!! KDUZ of Hutchinson wanted to do an interview with me. Lester Schuft of KDUZ conducted the interview with me about my country gospel C.D. My song, "The Halo and A Set of Golden Wings," the radio station played periodically. It was very much enjoyed! Then, I came up with an idea for the other four lyrics songs. I was going to contact Paramount Song of Nashville, I, sent them the four lyrics songs to see what they would do. It didn't take long and they responded, they contracted all four of them! For someone who had never written a lyrics song, this blew my mind! I, was again the Lyricist, they put music to my songs. I, could have a one piece band a three piece band or a five piece band with harmonizing. You had to pay for the bands. The four songs were: "Grandma's Squeaky Rocker," "I love My Country Grandpa," "Walking Down That Stumbling Road," "That Catchy Country Song." In time I received my C.D.'s and they were beautifully done from Paramount Songs in Nashville! I was blessed and they were Copy Written and put in The Library of Congress in Washington D.C.

HILLTOP Records wrote to me and wanted my song, "A Halo and a Set of Golden Wings," put on a C.D. where Lyricists and Musicians that were on it received a Gold Award! I, gave them permission to do that.

Paramount Songs contacted me in 2013, they wanted my song, "Walking down that Stumbling Road," on a Christmas C.D. called, "Catch a Rising Star." I, gave them permission to do that.

In 2016, I decided to get into family themed Bingo in the Winsted Community. We need a State License to conduct the themed Bingo at the Blue Note Ballroom in Winsted, MN. I now run and organize two family themed Bingo's, "Fishing with the Bunny" at Easter time and "Chicken Bingo" at Fall Harvest time. One business group has the non-profit 501 C and the other group helps run the event as well. We have concessions, Silent Auction, Dollar Raffle and 13 games of Bingo with consolation prizes and other prizes galore to give out!! They have all been successful and up to over 400 people attending! The money is shared between the two groups to help them with their needs!

I received a few years ago through Dominion Cares a business called Indeed, they find jobs for people. I was asked to submit a short article on how I take care of the elderly. My title was "Taking Care of the Elderly with a Positive Outcome." I was notified that I received a 5-star rating from Indeed out of all the people who submitted their versions!

I'm a very busy person still working with Dominion Cares, being a columnist with the Herald Journal in Winsted, MN. writing a story once a month, writing Momentous writings for the deceased, writing lyrics songs, and writing novels.

I continue organizing the two themed events, "Fishing with the Bunny and Chicken Bingo" helping non-profit businesses make money to use however they need to help them along the way!

I continually help or support in our Winsted community with the Festival Parade festivities, our church with Winstock Country Music Event for Holy Trinity Church and School and wherever need be in our community!

I received many calls from Citi of Books out of Albuquerque, NM. They were looking for me and wanted to be a part of my novel, "Inspirational Stories that Spark our Emotions and Touch the Heart and Soul." A scout had found my book at the Los Angeles, CA, book fair and found it of good quality reading material to pursue having their company name put in it and selling. After 3 years another Agency wanted to be a part of my book, how exciting!

Citi of Books Staff is going to make my book into a 3rd edition. The book will be going nationwide, countrywide, online, into bookstores, Barnes and Noble, Amazon, and Powell's, the largest bookstore in the U.S.A. I will be keeping my rights to my book. I find enjoyment in all my writing styles and plan to continue sharing my gifts that I was blessed with, now, and in the future ahead of me.

_____

Author signature.